MASTERING APPETITE

Keys to Eating and Staying Healthy

BLESSED CHARLES

ISBN: 9798878848206

DEDICATION

This book is dedicated to God

ACKNOWLEDGMENTS

I want to express my profound gratitude to the Almighty God for the strength and wisdom he gave me to put this great work together.

Almost I want to specifically appreciate my family for their support and love throughout this demanding period. More so, my parents and siblings for their encouragement and others who stood by me this period. I trust greater things are unfolding.

TABLE OF CONTENTS

Introduction With the help of "Mastering Appetite," readers can better understand and control their relationship with food. This enlightening book explores the complex relationship between the mind, body, and appetite, providing useful tips and deep understandings to help readers take back control of their eating patterns. In order to help readers develop mindful eating habits and strengthen their bond with their bodies and the food they eat, the book offers a whole toolset. From stress reduction methods and mindfulness practices to advice on diet planning and strategies for controlling food portions, each of the chapters of the book fortifies readers with actionable patterns to foster a balanced relationship with food.

Furthermore, "Mastering Appetite" explores the underlying reasons of overeating and emotional eating in addition to offering practical fixes. It gives readers the ability to uncover the underlying feelings and ideas that influence their dietary decisions, resulting in a significant mental change in favor of self-compassion, acceptance, and empowerment.

CHAPTER ONE

Understanding Appetite

Understanding appetite entails realizing the complex interactions between environmental, psychological, and physiological elements that affect our urge to eat, going beyond simple hunger.

Physical Indications:

Hunger Signals: It's critical to distinguish real physiological hunger from psychological or environmental clues. Experiencing an overall sense of emptiness, along with rumbling and stomach spasms, is typically indicative of true hunger.

Satiety: It's important to recognize the signals of fullness. This entails being aware of the little indicators that your body has had enough food.

Psychological Affects:

Emotional Eating: It's important to recognize the emotional

cues that cause eating when one isn't really hungry. In certain cases, emotions other than physical hunger might affect our urge to eat, such as stress, boredom, melancholy, or joy.

Cognitive Awareness: There is a relationship between your hunger and your mental state when you are aware of what and why you are eating.

Environmental Elements:

External Cues: Even when you're not hungry, external cues like the sight or scent of food might make you feel hungry. Making deliberate food choices may be aided by being aware of how these signals influence your eating patterns.

Social and Cultural Influences: It's important to understand how cultural customs and society standards affect your eating habits. It helps you in managing your hunger while navigating social settings.

Biochemical Elements:

Hormonal Regulation: The regulation of appetite is greatly influenced by hormones. For example, the hormones leptin and ghrelin indicate whether someone is hungry or full. People who are aware of these hormonal signals will be better able to control their eating habits.

Individual Variances: Understanding that each individual regulates their hunger differently enables a more tailored approach to understanding and controlling appetite.

Maintaining Nutrition Balance:

Desires and Nutrient inadequacies: It's important to comprehend how some desires might be caused by nutrient inadequacies. In addition to improving general health, a balanced diet facilitates better hunger control.

To grasp appetite, one must essentially take a holistic approach, learning to distinguish between bodily hungers and other stimuli, practicing mindfulness while eating, and taking into account the larger context of their surroundings and way of life. This thorough knowledge creates the groundwork for better eating practices and, in turn, a more balanced and satisfying existence.

Recognizing the Significance of Hunger

Gaining an understanding of the significance of appetite is essential to sustaining general health and leading a healthy lifestyle. Our food choices and nutritional intake are influenced by a complex interaction of physiological, psychological, and environmental elements that make up our appetite. Examining this idea in further detail shows its complex significance:

Intake of Nutrients:

Balanced Diet: Our natural appetite drives us to eat a range of nutrients that are necessary for our bodies to operate. A nutritious and well-balanced diet may be achieved by being aware of and responsive to hunger signals.

Micronutrient Adequacy: Sufficient intake of key vitamins and minerals is made possible by a healthy appetite, which in turn supports the best possible organ function, immune system response, and general vigor.

Equilibrium Energy:

Caloric Requirements: The appetite helps control calorie intake by bringing it into balance with the body's energy use. Sustaining energy levels and controlling weight depend on a balance between energy intake and expenditure.

Metabolic Health: By limiting overindulgence in calories, which may exacerbate metabolic conditions like obesity and insulin resistance, a well controlled appetite promotes metabolic health.

Mental Health:

Mood and Satisfaction: Psychological health is enhanced by recognizing and meeting hunger demands. Eating full meals may improve mood and give one a feeling of comfort and contentment.

Stress Reduction: Mindful eating techniques that are based on an awareness of hunger may be an effective means of lowering stress and fostering a healthy connection with food.

Prevention of Diseases:

illnesses Associated with Nutrition: Healthy eating habits and a balanced appetite help to avoid illnesses associated with nutrition, including diabetes, heart disease, and deficiencies.

Control of Inflammation: Some foods have the ability to increase or decrease inflammation. Appetite control may help people choose foods that reduce inflammation, which is beneficial for long-term health.

Adapting a lifestyle

Cultural Considerations: Being aware of one's hunger enables people to negotiate the social and cultural dimensions of eating. It makes it easier to modify eating habits to fit individual tastes, societal conventions, and social gatherings.

Prevention of Eating Disorders: By promoting a balanced attitude toward food and body image, a good knowledge of hunger may help avoid eating disorders.

Life Expectancy and Life Quality:

Healthy Aging: Maintaining a healthy appetite lowers the risk of age-related disorders and guarantees enough nourishment for body processes.

Cognitive Function: A well-controlled hunger and appropriate nutrition have a good impact on memory, cognitive function, and general brain health.

In conclusion, realizing the significance of appetite goes beyond making informed food decisions and includes factors related to overall quality of life, illness prevention, mental and physical health, and physical health. Developing a conscious knowledge of one's hunger enables people to make choices that are health-promoting and well-informed, which ultimately supports a balanced and all-encompassing way of life.

Getting Things Started in a Healthy Way of Life

Creating a healthy lifestyle requires thoughtful decision-making in all areas of your life and integrating virtuous habits. To start this process of transformation, follow these crucial steps:

Establish Your Objectives

Clearly state your goals for fitness and health. Setting clear objectives gives you direction in all areas of your life, including stress relief, improved diet, weight control, and physical exercise.

Make a Practical Plan:

Create a workable and realistic strategy to accomplish your objectives. Divide more ambitious goals into more doable chunks. To encourage consistency, take both immediate and long-term steps into consideration.

Create Healthful Eating Routines:

Prioritize eating a well-balanced diet that is high in whole grains, fruits, vegetables, lean meats, and healthy fats. Make nutrient-dense foods your first priority and limit processed and sugary meals. Moreover, portion control is essential.

Include Frequent Exercise:

Look for fun ways to work out, and try to be consistent. Regular physical exercise, such as cycling, running, walking, or attending fitness programs, is crucial for general health. Begin with pursuits you are really passionate about.

Make sleep a priority:

Make sure you get enough good sleep. Create a calming nighttime ritual and stick to a regular sleep schedule. For both physical and emotional health, getting enough sleep is essential.

Effective Stress Management:

Use stress-reduction strategies including meditation, deep breathing, and mindfulness. Long-term stress management requires finding joyous things to engage in and striking a balance between work and personal life.

Maintain Hydration:

Water should be consumed in moderation throughout the day. Many biological processes, including as digestion, vitamin absorption, and general cellular health, depend on enough hydration.

Develop Positive Relationships:

Be in the company of people who support you in leading a healthy lifestyle. Strong connections with others promote emotional health by lowering stress levels and creating a feeling of community.

Limit the amount of time spent on screens:

Pay attention to how much time you spend on electronics, particularly just before bed. Overuse of screens might affect the quality of sleep. Establish limits to keep things in a healthy balance.

Learn for Yourself:

Keep up with wellness and health-related topics. Keep learning about healthy eating, physical activity, and mental health. Having information gives you the ability to make wise choices.

Engage in Mindful Eating:

Observe what you eat and how you consume it. During meals, try not to be distracted, enjoy the tastes, and pay attention to your body's signals of hunger and fullness. Eating with awareness cultivates a more positive connection with food.

Frequent Health Examinations:

Make time for routine medical examinations to keep an eye on your general health. Timely intervention and prevention are made possible by the early identification of possible health conditions.

Honor accomplishments:

Celebrate and acknowledge your accomplishments. Reaching a fitness goal or making consistently healthy decisions are examples of accomplishments that should be acknowledged since they encourage good behavior.

Flexibility and Adaptability:

Be willing to change your strategy as needed. Because life is dynamic, things may change. Your capacity to adjust and be flexible will guarantee the sustainability of your healthy lifestyle.

You may create the foundation for a healthy lifestyle that supports mental, emotional, and physical well-being by implementing these actions into your everyday routine. Keep in mind that frequent tiny adjustments can result in long-lasting benefits.

The Significance of Appetite in Attaining General Welfare

A person's hunger plays a complex role in attaining total well-being that goes beyond simple nutrition. A person's ability to comprehend and efficiently control their hunger has a substantial impact on their physical, mental, and emotional well-being.

Intake and Balance of Nutrients:

Importance: The body uses appetite as a natural guide to determine what nutrients it needs. It affects the choice and consumption of many nutrients that are essential for general health.

Reaching Well-Being: Maintaining optimum body functioning and fostering general well-being is made possible by a well-controlled hunger, which stimulates the intake of a balanced diet high in vitamins, minerals, and important macronutrients.

Energy Governance:

Importance: Appetite balances caloric intake with energy expenditure in the body.

Attaining Well-Being: Eating a balanced diet helps with energy levels, weight control, and metabolic health—all of which are essential for general wellbeing.

Psychological and Emotional Wellbeing:

Importance: Emotional and psychological health are intimately related to appetite, which affects happiness and contentment.

Attaining Well-Being: Stress reduction and the development of a healthy connection with food may be achieved via mindful and fulfilling eating experiences that are fueled by a controlled hunger.

Prevention of Diseases:

Importance: Appetite management that is in good health helps avoid disorders linked to diet, including diabetes, obesity, and malnutrition.

Attaining Well-Being: A healthy diet that is directed by self-control over hunger is essential for preventing illness and promoting long-term wellbeing.

Influence of the Gut-Brain Axis:

Importance: The gut-brain axis facilitates communication between the brain and the digestive system, and hunger is a key component of this communication.

Attaining Well-Being: Digestion health and general well-being may be enhanced by a gut-brain axis that is in good working order and is supported by mindful eating and a balanced appetite.

Managing Hormones:

Significance: Hormones like ghrelin and leptin are involved in controlling hunger and regulating appetite.

Getting Well: Controlling hunger and understanding it affects metabolism, energy balance, and hormonal health in general. It also helps maintain hormonal balance.

Adapting a lifestyle:

Importance: People may modify their eating habits to suit social situations, cultural standards, and personal preferences when taking appetite into account.

Attaining Well-Being: Eating behaviors that are in line with cultural and personal contexts help people have a healthy relationship with food and promote their general well-being.

Mental Process:

Importance: Appetite influences proper nutrition, which has a good effect on memory, cognitive function, and general brain health.

Attaining Well-Being: A healthy brain improves mental clarity, attention, and emotional stability, all of which are factors in total cognitive well-being.

CHAPTER TWO

Knowledge of Appetite and Satisfaction

In order to have a positive connection with food and enhance general wellbeing, it is essential to comprehend hunger and contentment. It's learning to interpret the subtle cues your body gives you about being nourished and satisfied.

Differentiating Real Hunger:

Physical Cues: Feelings of emptiness, slight pain, and rumbling in the stomach are common physical indicators of genuine hunger.

Regular Meal Timing: By setting regular meal times, you may better coordinate your body's natural cycles of hunger, which will help you discern between true hunger and other cravings.

Conscious Eating Techniques:

Using the Senses: Eating mindfully is taking time to appreciate each mouthful and focusing on the tastes, textures, and scents. This increased consciousness makes it easier for you to identify fullness.

Eating Slowly: Eating at a slower pace helps your body recognize fullness more precisely, which helps you avoid overindulging and increase feelings of contentment.

Perceiving Cues of Hunger and Fullness:

Hunger Scale: Prior to and after meals, determine how hungry you are by using a hunger scale. Using this tool may help you become more aware of your body's cues.

Stopping at Satisfaction: Rather of overindulging in food, learn to stop eating when you are satisfied. This thoughtful strategy encourages a more positive connection with eating.

Comparing Physical and Emotional Hungry:

Understanding Emotional Triggers: Stress, boredom, and other non-physical signals are common causes of emotional hunger. You may address the underlying source of emotional triggers and stop using food as a coping technique by identifying them.

Assessing Cravings: Make a distinction between genuine physiological cravings and sentimental yearnings for certain meals. Making mindful dietary decisions is made easier when you are aware of the differences.

Nutritional Equilibrium for Satiety:

Nutrient-Rich Foods: Choose foods high in nutrients that provide you long-lasting energy and help you feel full. Durable contentment is facilitated by well-balanced meals that include a variety of proteins, fiber, and healthy fats.

Hydration: It's important to drink enough water to avoid confusing thirst with hunger. Water consumption throughout the day promotes general wellbeing.

Creating a Healthful Dining Space:

Reducing Distractions: Eat with attention and awareness while reducing outside distractions, such as devices. This improves your ability to recognize signs of hunger and fullness.

Pleasant Ambience: Establish a cheerful and delightful ambiance when dining, encouraging a feeling of contentment and gratification.

Considering Consumption Patterns:

Food Journaling: You may see trends in hunger, satisfaction, and emotional eating by keeping a food diary. Making educated changes to your eating habits is facilitated by this introspective process.

Honoring Personal Differences:

Personalized Approach: Be aware that everyone has different levels of hunger and contentment. Adopt a customized eating plan that fits your particular body type and way of living.

Being conscious of one's own hunger and contentment is an

ongoing practice. Focusing on these cues and using mindful eating techniques give you the ability to make decisions that fuel your body and foster a healthy, long-lasting connection with food.

How to pay attention to your body's signals of hunger and fullness

It takes awareness to tune into your body's subtle cues and pay attention to what it is telling you when it comes to hunger and contentment. The following concrete actions may help you become more adept at deciphering these signals:

Remain Aware During Meals:

Remain in the Now: Try to cut down on outside distractions while eating. Put electronics aside and focus on the process of eating. This improves your ability to understand how your body reacts.

Apply the Hunger Scale:

Before and After Meals: Use a hunger scale of 1 to 10, where 10 represents being too full and 1 represents being severely hungry. When you're feeling fairly hungry, try to start eating, and when you're satisfied enough, stop.

Chew Everything Well and Eat Slowly:

Savor Every Bite: Give each mouthful careful attention as you eat it. This helps with digestion and enables your body to communicate satiety before overindulging.

Take a Break and Check-In:

Mid-Meal Check-In: Take a moment throughout your meal to gauge how hungry you are right now. This enables you to modify your serving sizes in accordance with your body's responses.

Distinguish between Emotional and Physical Hungry:

Think About Triggers: Prior to grabbing a snack or a meal, consider what physical or mental signs are causing your hunger. Addressing emotional eating is made easier by this self-awareness.

Diversity and Well-Balanced Diet:

Include Nutrient-Rich meals: Opt for a range of meals that provide a well-balanced combination of fiber, healthy fats, and proteins. High-nutrient meals help you feel full and have energy for a long time.

Maintain Hydration:

Water Intake: Occasionally, dehydration might pass for appetite. Try drinking water first if you're feeling hungry in between meals and make sure you're staying properly hydrated throughout the day.

Observe Your Body's Natural Cues:

Stomach Contractions: Growling or stomach contractions are common signs of true physical hunger. Instead of focusing on outside signs, pay attention to these natural indications.

Use Your Intuition When Eating:

Trust Your Instincts: Rather than adhering to strict dietary guidelines, intuitive eating entails accepting your body's signals of hunger and fullness. Establish a relationship with your body's intuitive messages and learn to believe in your gut.

Observe and honor fullness signals.

Learn to identify the tiny cues that indicate fullness so that you can stop eating before you feel excessively full. Your brain needs some time to realize that you are content.

Consider Your Food Selections:

After-Meal Reflection: After a meal, pause to consider your feelings about various meals. Given how your body reacts to certain meals, this self-awareness might help you make better decisions in the future.

Consistent Eating Routine

Regular Meal Times: Set aside certain times for meals in order to have a consistent eating schedule. This promotes attentive eating practices and helps your body predict when you will feel hungry.

Through the regular integration of these activities, you may cultivate an enhanced consciousness about your body's signals of hunger and contentment. This mindful eating style eventually fosters a better connection with food and enhances general wellbeing.

Fulfilling Your Cravings vs. Nourishing Your Body

Maintaining a balanced and healthful eating habit requires knowing the difference between feeding your body and giving in to desires. Although they both influence our connection with food, they have separate functions and may have disparate effects on our general well-being.

Fueling Your Body:

The main objective of feeding your body is to provide it the vital nutrients it needs for healthy development, good operation, and general wellbeing.

Concentrate on Nutrient-Dense Foods: Make sure to eat a variety of entire, nutrient-dense foods, including whole grains, fruits, vegetables, lean meats, and healthy fats. A wide range of vitamins, minerals, and other essential nutrients may be found in these meals.

Benefits for Long-Term Health: Making nutrient-rich decisions a priority improves energy levels, promotes long-term health, and aids in preventing nutritional deficiencies and associated health problems.

Fulfilling Wants:

The goal of satisfying cravings is to meet certain needs related to flavor, texture, or pleasure. Many times, emotional, psychological, or sensory elements are connected to cravings.

A balanced approach emphasizes moderation even if it's necessary to enjoy the meals you want. Choose to treat yourself once in a while rather than include them in your diet on a daily basis.

Mindful Consumption: By carefully satisfying desires, you

may savor and appreciate tastes without going overboard. This fosters a positive connection with food and helps you avoid feeling guilty about indulging sometimes.

Finding a Balance:

Holistic Eating: A well-rounded strategy includes periodically giving in to desires as well as providing your body with nutrient-dense meals. By taking a balanced approach, you may satisfy your nutritional requirements and enjoy the joys of eating.

Preventing Deprivation: It may be difficult to establish a healthy and pleasant connection with food if you completely limit the meals you like. This can cause emotions of deprivation.

Emotional Awareness in Eating:

Recognizing Triggers: Stress or negative feelings may set up cravings, particularly for comfort foods. Instead than depending just on food for consolation, you may address the underlying reasons of your emotional eating behaviors by recognizing them.

Creating Healthy Coping Mechanisms: Reduce the dependency on food as the main coping strategy by developing healthy substitutes for handling stress or emotions, such as exercise, meditation, or joy-filled hobbies.

Conscious Eating Techniques:

Savoring Moments: Engage in mindful eating by enjoying every taste and the whole sensory experience that comes with your meal. This may increase contentment and lessen the propensity to overindulge in an effort to sate urges.

Listening to Your Body's Cues of Hungry and Fullness: Be aware of the signals your body sends forth. This awareness helps in differentiating between cravings that are fueled by outside forces and true hunger.

Creating a Satisfying Connection with Food:

Happy Eating: Make an effort to have a good and happy connection with eating. Accept the joy of feeding your body healthful meals and sometimes indulge in pleasures with awareness.

Reducing Guilt: A better attitude toward eating is facilitated by striking a balance between appetites and nutrients. This helps to minimize the guilt associated with food choices.

In conclusion, fulfilling desires and providing your body with nourishment are essential components of a well-rounded dietary plan. A healthy relationship with food is encouraged by carefully balancing these factors, which also supports mental and physical wellbeing.

CHAPTER THREE

Practices of Mindful Eating

By adopting a present-moment awareness of the tastes, textures, and sensations connected to food, mindful eaters give their whole focus to the eating experience. This method promotes a more deliberate and fulfilling relationship with eating, which benefits one's physical and emotional health. Key mindful eating techniques are as follows

Involve Your Senses:

Savor the Flavors: Take time to appreciate how each mouthful tastes. Give your meal some time to really enjoy its variety of tastes and sensations.

Eat Without Being Afraid:

No Screens or Multitasking: Steer clear of eating while using a computer, watching TV, or browsing through your phone. To increase awareness, concentrate just on the eating process.

Chew Carefully:

Chewing mindfully: Take your time and carefully chew your meal. This lets you feel the fullness of every mouthful in addition to helping with digestion.

Pay Attention to Your Body:

Cues for Hunger and Fullness: Pay attention to the cues your body sends forth. Eat till you're content, not too full, and quit when you're hungry.

Identify Your Emotional Triggers:

Emotional Eating Awareness: Recognize the emotional cues that might cause you to eat when you're not really hungry. Understanding these stressors enables you to deal with your feelings without eating.

Thank You for the Source:

Knowledge of Food Origin: Take into account the source of your food. Consider the work that went into making it and be thankful for the sustenance it offers.

Recognizing portion sizes:

Portion sizes should be considered while eating mindfully. Smaller bowls and plates may help reduce overindulgence and promote more deliberate eating.

Consume mindfully:

Purposeful Eating: Have a specific goal in mind when you eat. Think about the food's nutritional content and how it affects your overall health.

Conscientious Snacking:

Snack with Purpose: Mindful eating should also extend to snacks. To prevent mindless munching, intentionally choose and appreciate every meal.

Show Your Appreciation:

Gratitude for Food: Give thanks for the food that is currently on your plate for a minute. Consider the trip it took to get to you and the sustenance it offers.

Decrease Your Speed:

Pace Yourself: Take it slowly as you eat. Eating at a relaxed pace facilitates your body's ability to sense fullness.

In between bites, pause:

Take conscious breaks and set down your utensils in between meals. This breaks up the meal so that there is time for contemplation.

Absent Criticism:

Non-Judgmental Observation: Keep an impartial eye on your eating patterns. Instead of being critical of your eating choices, approach them with inquiry and self-compassion.

Develop Intentional Rituals:

Mealtime Rituals: Create customs around meals, such offering a quick grace or pausing to notice how your food looks. The mindful eating experience is enhanced by these customs.

By implementing these mindful eating techniques into your everyday routine, you may become more conscious of how you interact with food. By encouraging a more harmonious relationship between the mind and body, this mindful approach decreases overeating, increases contentment, and improves general wellbeing.

Methods for Consuming Meals Mindfully

Adopting a variety of practices that center on being completely present and attentive throughout the eating experience is part of practicing mindful meal consumption. These methods are meant to heighten consciousness, cultivate a healthy relationship with food, and encourage a closer connection between the body and mind. The following are many methods for mindful meal consumption:

Conscious Breathing:

Technique: Take a few deep breaths to focus yourself before starting your meal. Give your breathing some attention and give it time to calm and deepen. This promotes awareness of the here and now.

Concise Observation:

Method: Examine the colors, forms, and arrangement of your food before biting into it. Note the textures on your plate, as well as any steam or smells emanating from it.

Conscientious Appreciation:

Method: Give thanks for the dinner. Think about how much work went into getting the ingredients and cooking it. This cultivates gratitude for the food received and an optimistic outlook.

Conscious Plating:

Technique: Take the time to plate your food thoughtfully. Arrange it in an aesthetically pleasing way, enhancing the visual appeal and inviting a more mindful eating experience.

Chew Mindfully:

Technique: Chew each bite thoroughly, paying attention to the taste and texture. Put down your utensils between bites to focus on chewing before taking the next bite.

Slow Down Your Pace:

Technique: Eat at a slower pace. Savor each bite and give your body the chance to register fullness, preventing overeating and enhancing enjoyment.

Involve Your Senses:

Technique: Utilize all your senses during the meal. Notice the crunch, taste, and aroma of your food. Engaging multiple senses enhances the overall eating experience.

Mindful Silence:

Technique: Consider incorporating moments of silence during the meal. This allows you to eat without distractions and fosters a deeper connection to the act of eating.

Mindful Check-Ins:

Technique: Pause at intervals to check in with your hunger and fullness levels. Assess how your body is feeling, and adjust your eating pace accordingly.

Awareness of Emotions:

Technique: Pay attention to any emotions that arise during the meal. Notice if you're eating due to stress, boredom, or genuine hunger. This awareness helps address emotional eating patterns.

Gratitude Journaling:

Technique: Keep a gratitude journal dedicated to your meals. Write down what you are thankful for regarding each meal, fostering a positive and mindful mindset.

Conscious Swallowing:

Technique: Be mindful of the act of swallowing. Notice the sensations as the food moves through your mouth and throat. This helps maintain focus on the eating process.

In between bites, pause:

Technique: Put your utensils down or take a moment to breathe between bites. This deliberate pause encourages mindful eating and prevents rushing through the meal.

Mindful Tea or Coffee Rituals:

Technique: If you consume beverages with your meals, create a mindful ritual around them. Sip slowly, savoring the flavors, and being fully present in the moment.

Mindful Cleanup:

Technique: Extend mindfulness to the post-meal experience. Take your time cleaning up, appreciating the effort that went into the meal preparation and expressing gratitude for the nourishment received.

By incorporating these mindful meal consumption techniques, you can elevate your eating experience, foster a deeper connection with your food, and promote overall well-being.

The Connection Between Mindfulness and Healthy Choices

The connection between mindfulness and healthy choices is profound, influencing various aspects of well-being, including physical health, emotional balance, and overall lifestyle. Here are key ways in which mindfulness contributes to making healthier choices:

Increased Awareness:

Mindful Presence: Mindfulness involves being fully present in the current moment. This heightened awareness allows individuals to notice thoughts, emotions, and bodily sensations, fostering a deeper understanding of their internal states.

Understanding Cravings and Habits:

Observing Triggers: Mindfulness helps individuals observe cravings and habitual patterns without judgment. By identifying triggers and understanding the underlying reasons for certain choices, it becomes easier to make conscious decisions.

Emotional Regulation:

Managing Stress and Emotions: Mindfulness practices, such as meditation and deep breathing, contribute to emotional regulation. This, in turn, reduces the likelihood of turning to unhealthy food or habits as a coping mechanism during times of stress or emotional turmoil.

Improved Decision-Making:

Cognitive Clarity: Mindfulness enhances cognitive clarity and decision-making abilities. This mental clarity allows individuals to make healthier choices by considering the long-term impact of their decisions on their well-being

Enhanced Self-Control:

Resisting Impulses: Mindfulness cultivates self-awareness and self-regulation, empowering individuals to resist impulsive behaviors, particularly those that may be detrimental to their health.

Intuitive Eating:

Listening to Body Signals: Mindfulness encourages intuitive eating, where individuals listen to their body's hunger and fullness cues rather than following external cues or rigid diet plans.

Breaking Automatic Pilot:

Interrupting Unconscious Habits: Mindfulness disrupts

automatic pilot mode, allowing individuals to pause and consider their choices rather than succumbing to habitual, often unhealthy, behaviors.

Reduced Stress-Related Eating:

Coping with Stress: Mindfulness practices provide effective tools for managing stress. By addressing stressors mindfully, individuals are less likely to resort to unhealthy eating habits as a way to cope.

Mindful Movement and Exercise:

Physical Well-being: Mindful movement, such as yoga or mindful walking, can enhance the connection between the mind and body. This holistic approach contributes to a more positive attitude towards exercise and physical activity.

Conscious Eating Techniques:

Savoring Each Bite: Mindful eating involves savoring each bite, being fully present during meals, and paying attention to hunger and fullness cues. This practice promotes healthier food choices and prevents overeating.

Increased Gratitude:

Appreciation for Nourishment: Mindfulness cultivates gratitude, leading individuals to appreciate the nourishment provided by healthy food choices. This positive mindset reinforces a preference for foods that contribute to well-being.

Mindful Stress Reduction Programs:

Holistic Health Approaches: Mindfulness-based stress reduction (MBSR) programs often incorporate healthy lifestyle components. Participants learn to integrate mindfulness into various aspects of their lives, including nutrition and physical activity.

Long-Term Behavioral Change:

Sustainable Choices: Mindfulness supports sustainable, long-term behavioral change. Rather than adopting short-term fixes, individuals are more likely to embrace lasting healthy habits rooted in mindful awareness.

In summary, mindfulness creates a powerful foundation for making healthier choices by fostering awareness, emotional regulation, and a deep connection between mind and body. By integrating mindfulness into daily life, individuals can approach their well-being with a more conscious and intentional mindset.

CHAPTER FOUR

Nutrient-Rich Eating

Nutrient-rich eating involves selecting foods that are dense in essential nutrients, providing a wide array of vitamins, minerals, proteins, healthy fats, and carbohydrates without an excess of empty calories. This dietary approach focuses on nourishing the body with optimal nutrition, supporting overall health and well-being. Here's an in-depth exploration of nutrient-rich eating:

Diverse and Colorful Fruits and Vegetables:

Vitamins and Minerals: Incorporating a variety of fruits and vegetables ensures a diverse intake of vitamins (such as vitamin C, A, and folate) and minerals (like potassium and magnesium) crucial for various bodily functions.

Antioxidants: The vibrant colors in fruits and vegetables often indicate the presence of antioxidants, which help combat oxidative stress and support cellular health.

Whole Grains:

Fiber and B Vitamins: Whole grains, such as quinoa, brown rice, and oats, provide a rich source of dietary fiber and B vitamins. Fiber supports digestive health, while B vitamins contribute to energy metabolism and overall well-being.

Lean Proteins:

Complete Proteins: Lean protein sources like poultry, fish, beans, and legumes offer essential amino acids necessary for building and repairing tissues, supporting muscle health, and regulating various physiological processes.

Iron and Zinc: Lean meats provide iron and zinc, crucial for oxygen transport in the blood and immune function.

Healthy Fats:

Omega-3 Fatty Acids: Foods rich in omega-3 fatty acids, such as fatty fish (salmon, mackerel) and flaxseeds, support heart health, reduce inflammation, and contribute to brain function.

Monounsaturated and Polyunsaturated Fats: Olive oil, avocados, and nuts contain heart-healthy monounsaturated and polyunsaturated fats, which help maintain cholesterol levels.

Dairy or Dairy Alternatives:

Calcium and Vitamin D: Dairy products or fortified dairy alternatives are excellent sources of calcium and vitamin D, essential for bone health and overall immune function.

Legumes and Pulses:

Plant-Based Proteins: Beans, lentils, and chickpeas provide plant-based protein, dietary fiber, and a range of vitamins and minerals. They contribute to satiety and support digestive health.

Nuts and Seeds:

Nutrient Density: Nuts and seeds are dense in essential nutrients, including healthy fats, protein, vitamins, and minerals. They are also rich in antioxidants, promoting heart health and reducing inflammation.

Low-Fat Dairy or Dairy Alternatives:

Protein and Calcium: Low-fat dairy or fortified dairy alternatives supply protein, calcium, and other nutrients crucial for bone health and overall well-being.

Hydration with Water:

Optimal Hydration: Water is essential for digestion, nutrient absorption, and overall hydration. Choosing water as the primary beverage supports optimal bodily functions.

Portion Control:

Balanced Intake: Nutrient-rich eating involves mindful portion control. Balancing the intake of different food groups ensures a diverse range of nutrients without overloading on any specific component.

Minimizing Processed Foods:

Whole Food Emphasis: Minimizing processed and refined foods helps prioritize whole, nutrient-dense options. Whole foods generally contain a broader spectrum of nutrients compared to their processed counterparts.

Individualized Nutrition:

Personalized Approach: Recognizing individual nutritional needs allows for a personalized approach to nutrient-rich eating. Factors like age, activity level, and health conditions influence dietary requirements.

Meal Planning and Preparation:

Consistency: Planning and preparing meals in advance facilitate consistent nutrient-rich eating. This approach reduces reliance on convenience foods and supports the inclusion of a variety of wholesome ingredients.

Regular Check-ups and Adjustments:

Health Monitoring: Regular health check-ups and assessments allow individuals to monitor their nutritional status and make adjustments to their diet based on changing needs or deficiencies.

In essence, nutrient-rich eating emphasizes a well-balanced and diverse diet, focusing on whole, minimally processed foods to provide the body with the essential nutrients it needs for optimal functioning and overall health.

Building a Foundation of Nutrient-Dense Foods

Building a foundation of nutrient-dense foods is essential for supporting overall health and well-being. Here are practical ways to incorporate nutrient-dense foods into your diet and establish a solid foundation for optimal nutrition:

Emphasize Whole Foods:

Prioritize whole, minimally processed meals. Opt for fresh fruits, veggies, whole grains, lean proteins, and healthy fats. These foods preserve their original nutrients and give a wide range of health advantages.

Colorful Plate Approach:

Aim for a bright meal by incorporating a range of fruits and vegetables. Different hues frequently imply varied nutrients, so including a rainbow of food guarantees a diversity of vitamins, minerals, and antioxidants.

Include Lean Proteins:

Choose lean protein sources such as chicken, fish, tofu, lentils, and low-fat dairy. These solutions deliver necessary amino acids and assist muscular health without excessive saturated fats.

Prioritize Plant-Based Foods:

Increase your diet of plant-based foods including beans, lentils, nuts, seeds, and whole grains. Plant-based choices are rich in fiber, vitamins, and minerals, contributing to overall wellness.

Select Whole Grains:

Opt for healthy grains like brown rice, quinoa, oats, and whole wheat. Whole grains include fiber, B vitamins, and minerals, improving intestinal health and lasting energy.

Incorporate Healthy Fats:

Consume foods high in avocados, almonds, olive oil, and fatty seafood as well as other forms of healthy fats. These fats aid in the absorption of fat-soluble vitamins, cognitive function, and heart health.

Cut Down on Added Sugars:

Eat less of the meals and drinks that have a lot of added sugar. To quell sweet cravings and cut down on manufactured sweets, go for naturally sweet foods like fruits.

Drink Water to Remain Hydrated:

Make water your main hydration option. Maintaining proper hydration promotes general health and may aid in limiting the intake of sugar- or calorie-laden beverages.

Arrange Well-Balanced Meals

Prepare meals that are well-balanced and include a range of veggies, healthy fats, carbs, and proteins. This guarantees that each meal has a balanced intake of nutrients.

Examine the nutrition labels:

Learn how to read nutrition labels so that you may make wise decisions. Seek for foods with minimal amounts of salt, added sugars, and saturated fats and good nutritional value.

Use Portion Control Techniques:

Pay attention to portion proportions to prevent overindulging. You may enjoy a range of meals without consuming more calories when you eat in moderation.

Add dairy or dairy substitutes:

Include dairy products with reduced fat or fortified dairy substitutes to get calcium and vitamin D, which are vital for healthy bones.

Preparing Meals for Convenience:

To guarantee that you have access to nutrient-dense foods, particularly on hectic days, plan and prepare your meals in advance. Having healthy meals on hand helps one become less dependent on fast food and convenience.

Select Nutrient-Dense Foods:

Snack on nutrient-dense foods like almonds, hummus, veggies, and fresh fruit. These snacks provide you more nutrients without adding unnecessary calories.

Change Up Your Food Selections:

Change up the foods you eat to add some diversity to your diet. A varied diet promotes overall nutritional sufficiency because various foods provide varying amounts of nutrients.

Speak with an Expert in Nutrition:

To develop a customized plan suited to your unique dietary requirements and health objectives, think about speaking with a licensed dietitian or nutritionist.

Establishing a base of nutrient-dense meals requires

deliberate and thoughtful decision-making where the nutritional content of your diet is given top priority. You may create a strong dietary base that supports health and wellbeing by implementing these habits into your everyday routine.

Appropriate Foods for Long-Term Energy

Maintaining a healthy diet is essential to having enough energy throughout the day. Combining dietary fiber, micronutrients, and macronutrients is part of a well-rounded strategy. When attempting to achieve a balanced diet that encourages prolonged energy, consider the following important factors:

Complex Glycosomics:

Whole Grains: Opt for whole grains including whole wheat, quinoa, brown rice, and oats. These provide complex carbs that steadily deliver energy while preserving steady blood sugar levels.

Foods High in Protein:

Lean Proteins: Consume low-fat dairy products, fish, chicken, beans, lentils, and tofu, among other lean protein sources. Protein helps maintain the health of your muscles and prolongs feelings of fullness.

Good Fats:

Consume foods high in monounsaturated and polyunsaturated fats, such as avocados, nuts, seeds, and olive oil. These fats enhance general wellbeing and provide long-lasting energy.

Vibrantly colored fruits and veggies:

Nutrient-Dense Options: Arrange a rainbow of vibrant fruits and veggies on your plate. They boost general health and energy generation by supplying vital vitamins, minerals, and antioxidants.

Foods High in Fiber:

Whole Plant Foods: Go for fruits, vegetables, whole grains, legumes, and other foods rich in dietary fiber. Fiber promotes a sustained sensation of fullness, facilitates digestion, and helps control blood sugar levels.

Well-Balanced Meals:

Combination of Nutrients: To create meals that are balanced, combine proteins, fats, and carbs. Over time, this combination aids in delivering a consistent flow of energy.

Drinking plenty of water

Water as the Main Drink: Drink enough water to be well hydrated. Sustained energy depends on maintaining the right fluid balance since dehydration may cause weariness.

Smart Snack:

Nutrient-Dense Snacks: Choose healthy snacks like fresh fruit, Greek yogurt, or a handful of almonds in between meals. These foods give you a rapid energy boost without sending your blood sugar skyrocketing.

Limit Your Sugar Intake:

Minimize Added Sugars: Cut down on the amount of sugar-rich meals and drinks that you consume. Although they could bring you a temporary energy boost, they often cause a crash that leaves you tired.

Typical Meals:

Consistent Eating Routine: Keep a regular eating routine that includes well-balanced meals and snacks. This constancy maintains energy levels throughout the day and aids with blood sugar regulation.

Moderate Use of Tea and Coffee:

Coffee and tea may provide you a short-term energy boost, but you should only use them occasionally to prevent dependency and possible energy dumps.

Take Omega-3 Fatty Acids Into Account:

Include foods high in omega-3 fatty acids, such as flaxseeds and fatty fish (salmon, mackerel). These fats promote long-lasting energy and brain function.

Iron-Dense Foods:

Lean Meats, Legumes, and Leafy Greens: Make sure that you are getting enough iron from foods such as these. Iron aids in the movement of oxygen, which is necessary for the synthesis of energy.

Supplements Made Whole Foods:

Whole Foods: Whenever feasible, get your nutrition from whole foods instead than only taking pills. A rich matrix of nutrients included in whole meals collaborate to promote the best possible energy metabolism.

Think About Personal Needs:

Personalized Approach: When creating a balanced food plan, take into account personal characteristics like age, degree of exercise, and medical concerns. A tailored strategy guarantees that your dietary requirements meet your specific demands.

In conclusion, a balanced diet for long-term energy entails consuming a range of foods high in nutrients, drinking enough of water, and adhering to a regular meal schedule. Making whole, minimally processed meals a priority can help you provide your body the nutrition it needs for long-lasting energy and general health.

CHAPTER FIVE

Drinking Enough Water for Health

The vital practice of maintaining an appropriate fluid balance in the body to promote general well-being is known as "hydration for health." Sufficient hydration is essential for many physiological processes and promotes the best possible physical and mental well-being. Key elements of hydration for health are as follows:

Water as an Essential Mineral:

Every cell, tissue, and organ in the body needs water to operate properly, making it one of the basic nutrients.

How to Spot Dehydration Signs:

Thirst, Dark Urine, and Fatigue: Recognizing the symptoms of dehydration, such as these three indicators, encourages people to drink more fluids.

Moderate Hydration Techniques:

Not Just Water: Other drinks, fruits, and vegetables also add to total fluid consumption, even though water is the main source of hydration. It's important to have a balanced approach to staying hydrated.

Staying Hydrated During the Day:

Regular Consumption: It is more beneficial to regularly consume water throughout the day as opposed to ingesting huge quantities at once. This strategy aids in maintaining consistent amounts of water.

It's important to pay attention to individual demands, be careful of fluid consumption, and acknowledge the significance of water in maintaining the body's essential processes when it comes to maintaining sufficient hydration for health. A well hydrated body is better able to sustain ideal health and operate at peak performance.

The Benefits of Adequate Hydration for Health

Staying well hydrated is essential for preserving general health and wellbeing. The following are some major health benefits of adequate hydration:

Function of Cells:

Water is necessary for individual cells to perform well in cellular processes. It promotes the general health of cells by facilitating the movement of nutrients, chemical processes, and the elimination of waste.

Control of Temperature:

Heat Dissipation: Sweating is a natural way for the body to release heat when it is properly hydrated. In order to avoid overheating during physical activity and in hot surroundings, this cooling system is essential.

Mental Process:

Mental Acuity: Hydration is essential for proper cognitive performance. Dehydration may cause trouble focusing, memory issues, and a reduction in attentiveness.

Levels of Energy:

Metabolic Efficiency: Drinking enough water helps your body break down nutrients for energy. It also promotes metabolic processes. Feelings of exhaustion and decreased physical performance may be caused by dehydration.

Lubricating joints:

Joint and Tissue Health: Drinking enough water keeps joints lubricated and provides support for flexibility and cushioning. This is crucial for maintaining general joint health and avoiding damage.

gastrointestinal health

Encouraging Digestion: Water is essential for nutrient absorption and digestion. It facilitates food digestion and the digestive system as a whole.

Heart Conditions:

Blood Volume and Circulation: Sustaining blood volume through proper hydration promotes effective circulation.

This guarantees the heart's ability to pump blood efficiently, which is critical for cardiovascular health.

Kidney Function:

Waste Elimination: Hydration facilitates the kidneys' ability to expel toxins and waste materials through urine. Drinking enough water promotes overall kidney health and helps prevent kidney stones.

Skin Conditions:

Skin Hydration: By preserving moisture levels, adequate hydration promotes healthy skin. Dehydration can aggravate certain skin conditions and cause dry skin.

Controlling Weight:

Appetite Control: Drinking enough water can help control appetite and stop overindulging. Occasionally, the body may misinterpret thirst for hunger, resulting in the consumption of extra calories.

Function of Muscles:

Preventing Cramps: Sufficient hydration is essential for healthy muscle contraction. During physical activity, muscle cramps and stiffness can become more common when dehydrated.

Support for the Immune System:

Immune system function is aided by the lymphatic system, which is supported by hydration. Immune cells and antibodies circulate more easily when there is proper fluid balance.

Preventing Problems Caused by Dehydration:

Heat-Related Illnesses: Especially in hot weather or after strenuous physical activity, staying properly hydrated is crucial to avoiding heat-related illnesses like heat exhaustion and heatstroke.

Balancing Electrolytes:

Sodium and Potassium Regulation: Hydration helps balance electrolytes, such as sodium and potassium, which are crucial for nerve function, muscle contractions, and maintaining fluid balance.

Reducing the Risk of Chronic Conditions:

Associated with Dehydration: Chronic conditions such as urinary tract infections and constipation may be associated with inadequate hydration. Proper fluid intake can contribute to the prevention of these issues.

Enhanced Exercise Performance:

Reducing Fatigue: Staying hydrated during exercise is essential for optimal performance. Dehydration can lead to early fatigue, decreased endurance, and impaired physical function.

Ensuring proper hydration is a foundational element of maintaining good health. It supports numerous physiological processes, from cellular function to cognitive performance, and plays a vital role in preventing various health issues associated with dehydration.

Hydration Impacts Appetite

Hydration can have an impact on appetite, and understanding this relationship is essential for maintaining overall health. Here are ways in which hydration influences appetite:

Thirst vs. Hunger:

Misinterpretation: Sometimes, the body can misinterpret signals of thirst as hunger. Staying well-hydrated helps differentiate between true hunger and the need for fluids, preventing unnecessary calorie intake.

Appetite Suppression:

Hydration as a Natural Appetite Suppressant: Drinking water before meals can create a feeling of fullness, naturally suppressing appetite and reducing the likelihood of overeating during a meal.

Energy Levels and Appetite:

Dehydration-Related Fatigue: Dehydration can lead to fatigue and low energy levels. In response, the body may signal an increase in appetite as a way to obtain energy. Staying hydrated helps maintain energy levels and may reduce the desire to eat.

Metabolic Processes:

Optimal Metabolism: Hydration supports metabolic processes, including the breakdown of nutrients for energy. Proper metabolism contributes to a more balanced appetite regulation.

Water Content in Foods:

Hydrating Foods: Foods with high water content, such as fruits and vegetables, can contribute to overall hydration and provide a sense of fullness, potentially impacting appetite.

Electrolyte Balance:

Sodium and Thirst: Electrolyte balance, particularly sodium levels, can influence thirst. Hydration helps maintain electrolyte balance, reducing excessive thirst that can be misconstrued as hunger.

Meal Satisfaction:

Hydration and enjoyment: Proper hydration during meals may boost the enjoyment obtained from the eating experience, perhaps lessening the impulse to snack or overeat later.

Dehydration-Induced Snacking:

Compensatory munching: Dehydration could lead to compensatory munching as a reaction to low energy levels or feelings of weakness. Staying hydrated may help dampen these signals and lessen the chance of needless eating.

Mindful Eating:

Promoting Mindful Choices: Adequate water enhances mindful eating behaviors. Being in a hydrated condition helps people to make more mindful and purposeful meal decisions, minimizing impulsive and perhaps harmful eating.

Hydration and Exercise:

Fluid Balance During activity: Hydration before, during, and after activity is vital. Dehydration during physical activity might contribute to heightened sensations of hunger post-exercise. Proper fluid consumption helps maintain a balanced appetite response.

Reducing Liquid Calories:

Choosing Water over Caloric drinks: Opting for water instead of sugary or caloric drinks may assist reduce total calorie consumption. Liquid calories from drinks may sometimes lead to overindulgence in calories without giving rise to feelings of fullness.

Foods High in Water and Fullness:

Including meals rich in Water: Eating meals rich in water, such as salads, stews, and soups, will help you stay hydrated overall and feel fuller longer, which may have an effect on your appetite.

It's important to remember that everyone has different demands for hydration, and that hydration affects hunger in different ways depending on a variety of variables like age, activity level, climate, and health. A more thoughtful and balanced approach to eating may be achieved by including meals high in water, paying attention to indications of thirst, and maintaining appropriate hydration.

CHAPTER SIX

Developing Nutritious Food Habits

Developing a balanced lifestyle, supplying vital nutrients, and promoting general well-being are all part of developing good eating habits. An extended summary of how to create and maintain good eating practices is provided below:

Consciously Consuming Food:

Savoring Every meal: To cultivate mindful eating, focus on the tastes, textures, and fragrances of each meal. This strategy encourages a closer connection with the eating process and aids in reducing overindulgence.

Well-Balanced Meals:

Including Nutrient Groups: Prepare meals that are well-balanced and contain a range of fruits, vegetables, healthy fats, and carbs. This guarantees a wide range of nutrients for optimum well-being.

Control of Portion:

The key is moderation: manage your portion sizes to prevent overindulging. To maintain a healthy balance, use smaller plates, pay attention to signals of hunger and fullness, and be conscious of serving amounts.

Continual Meal Routine:

Consistency: Make sure you stick to a regular mealtime routine. This lessens the chance of making bad eating choices by preventing excessive hunger and assisting in blood sugar regulation.

Drinking plenty of water

Make water your main beverage. Water is a staple. Maintaining proper hydration facilitates healthy digestion, absorption of nutrients, and general wellbeing. Limit your consumption of sugar-filled beverages and caffeine.

The Focus on Whole Foods:

Reducing the Amount of Processed Foods: Give preference to whole, less processed foods over refined or highly processed ones. Whole foods improve general health by retaining more nutrients.

Variety in Food Selections:

Eating a Rainbow: Vary your diet to include a range of vibrant fruits and vegetables. Various hues often represent different nutrients, offering a multitude of health advantages.

Minimize Salt and Added Sugars:

Examining labels: Pay attention to salt and added sugars in packaged goods. Reducing these may improve general wellbeing and heart health.

Preparing Meals:

Planning Ahead: To guarantee that there are healthy alternatives available, plan and prepare meals in advance. Having wholesome meals on hand helps one become less dependent on fast food and convenience.

Paying Attention to Hunger Cues

Eating Intuitively: Recognize when your body is hungry and satisfied. Rather to giving in to outside indications or emotional impulses, eat when you're hungry and quit when you're content.

wholesome snacking

Nutrient-Dense Snacks: Select high-nutrient snacks such as almonds, hummus-topped veggies, or fresh fruit. Nutritious snacks enhance overall nutrition without consuming too many calories.

Foods with High Processing: Limiting

Minimize Ultra-Processed Items: Cut down on the amount of highly processed foods that include artificial substances, preservatives, and additives. Choosing authentic, whole foods will improve their nutritional worth.

Investigating Cuisine:

Trying New dishes: Investigate and test out various culinary techniques and dishes. This adds excitement to meals, which facilitates sticking to a balanced eating schedule.

Social Eating with Family:

Encouraging Good Eating Practices: Promote good eating practices in your social groups or family. A supportive community that includes sharing wholesome meals promotes the maintenance of good lifestyle choices.

Learning for Yourself:

Comprehending Nutrition: Remain aware of dietary recommendations and make well-informed decisions. Making better judgments is made possible when you are aware of a food's nutritional worth.

Not Deprivation, But Moderation:

Enjoying delicacies Occasionally: Moderately allow oneself to indulge in delicacies from time to time. Giving up all of your favorite meals might cause cravings and make it difficult to maintain good habits.

Customized Method:

Personalized Nutrition: Admit that people have different demands when it comes to nutrition. Take into account variables like age, degree of physical activity, and medical issues to customize your eating patterns to meet your specific needs.

Frequent Medical Examinations:

Monitoring Nutritional Status: Make time for routine medical examinations to keep an eye on your nutritional status and alter your diet as necessary in response to evolving requirements or shortfalls.

You may create and maintain healthy eating habits that support general wellbeing and contribute to a balanced, sustainable lifestyle by implementing these practices into your daily routine.

Realistic Strategies for Creating Consistent Meal Routines

Setting up regular meal schedules is crucial for maintaining steady energy levels, promoting general health, and avoiding extreme hunger, which may result in unhealthful food selections. The following are doable strategies for creating and maintaining regular meal schedules:

Establish Normative Meal Times:

The secret is consistency: Set aside certain times for breakfast, lunch, supper, and snacks, and make an effort to adhere to these schedules every day. Developing a routine promotes healthy digestion and helps control appetite

Organize Your Meals:

Meal Planning: Schedule your meals, along with your snacks, in advance. Planning your meals in advance might help you avoid impulsive, less nourishing decisions and choose better ones.

Add a Well-Blended Mixture:

Carbs, Proteins, and Fats: Make sure that a variety of carbs, proteins, and good fats are included in each meal. This combo encourages fullness and long-lasting energy.

Never Forget Breakfast:

Start the Day Off Right: Consume a well-balanced breakfast to provide vital nutrients and boost your metabolism. A healthy breakfast reduces the risk of overeating later in the day and helps to normalize blood sugar levels.

Consciously Consuming Food:

Be Present at Meals: Engage in mindful eating by putting all of your attention on the process of eating. This may encourage more purposeful eating by raising your awareness of hunger and fullness signals.

Stay Hydrated All Day

Water with Meals: To aid with digestion and hydration, have water with your meals. Preventing the impulse to eat due to dehydration may also be achieved by maintaining proper hydration.

Add Nutritious Snacks:

Nutrient-Dense Snacks: Make time for nutritious snacks like almonds, yogurt, or fresh fruit in between meals. These foods help stave off severe hunger and provide prolonged energy.

Pay Attention to Your Body:

Cues for Hunger and Fullness: Pay attention to the signals

your body sends forth. Rather of following set meal times, eat when you're hungry and quit when you're full.

Prevent Severe Hungry:

Regular Intervals: To avoid acute hunger, avoid going for extended periods of time without eating. A stable intake of nutrients is maintained throughout the day with the aid of regular, well-planned meals and snacks.

Restrict Grazing:

Structured Eating: Although snacks are beneficial, try to limit your day's worth of grazing. Well-planned meals and snacks can encourage balanced eating and discourage mindless nibbling.

Incorporate High-Fibre Foods:

Whole Grains, Fruits, and Vegetables: High-fiber foods help you feel satisfied longer. Incorporate fruits, veggies, and healthy grains into your meals to help maintain a regular meal schedule.

Variety in Cuisine:

Diverse Meals: To avoid boredom, include a range of items into your meals. Eating a varied diet guarantees you get a broad spectrum of nutrients and enhances your enjoyment of meals.

Establish sensible objectives:

Achievable Changes: Make frequent mealtimes a realistic aim by setting reasonable expectations. Make long-term sustainable adjustments to your habit by introducing them gradually.

Social and familial support:

Promote Meal Routines: If at all feasible, take part in creating a regular meal schedule with your family or friends. Mealtime practices that are shared may promote responsibility and mutual support.

Make a Special Occasion Plan:

Flexibility: Be adaptable on exceptional occasions even if routine is crucial. Give yourself permission to indulge in exceptional meals guilt-free, and then go back to your routine.

Give Nutrient-Dense Foods Priority:

Whole Foods: Make nutrient-dense, whole foods a priority while preparing meals. These meals support general health and wellbeing by supplying vital vitamins and minerals.

Observe and Modify:

Evaluate and Modify: Continually evaluate your eating habits and make necessary adjustments. Your meal schedule may need to be adjusted in response to changes in your activity level, way of life, or health.

Through the use of these doable tactics, you may create and preserve consistent meal schedules that support well-rounded dietary habits, prolonged energy, and general health.

Methods for Including Variation in a Balanced Diet

To ensure that you get a wide range of vital nutrients, you must include diversity in your diet for balanced nutrition. Here's a closer look at several strategies for adding diversity and achieving a balanced diet:

Variety in Food Groups:

All Food categories Should Be Included: Include items from all of the main food categories, such as grains, fruits, vegetables, dairy products, and meats. Nutrients specific to each dietary type are essential for general health.

Vibrantly colored fruits and veggies:

Colors High in Nutrients: Choose a range of vibrant fruits and vegetables. Diverse antioxidant molecules, vitamins, and minerals are often indicated by different colors. Aim for a rainbow of fruit to get the most nutritional value.

Complete Grains:

Investigate Different Grains: Pick a range of whole grains, including barley, quinoa, brown rice, and oats. A variety of nutrients, such as fiber, vitamins, and minerals, are provided by each grain, all of which support healthy digestion and general wellbeing.

Trim Proteins:

A variety of lean protein sources, such as fish, chicken, beans, lentils, tofu, and nuts, should be included in your diet. Different protein sources provide different amino acids that are necessary for the health of muscles and the body as a whole.

Good Fats:

Sources of Good Fats: Include healthy fats from foods such as olive oil, nuts, seeds, and avocados. These fats support healthy heart and brain function as well as the uptake of fat-soluble vitamins.

Plant-Based Substitutes:

Investigate Plant-Based Options: Include plant-based proteins in your diet, such as beans, lentils, and soy products. Plant-based substitutes are higher in nutrients and may be better for heart health.

Dairy products or substitutes:

Sources of Calcium and Vitamin D: Dairy products or fortified dairy substitutes are good sources of these minerals, which are important for healthy bones. Yogurt, milk, and fortified plant-based milks are among the options.

Omega-3 Fatty Acids in Seafood:

Add Omega-3 fatty acids to your seafood by include fatty fish like trout, salmon, and mackerel. These fats improve brain function, lower inflammation, and promote heart health.

Spices and Herbs:

Taste Diversity: To give your food more taste, try experimenting with different herbs and spices. Herbs contribute extra antioxidants and health-promoting substances to food in addition to improving flavor.

Foods that have undergone fermentation:

Make Probiotic-Rich Food Selections: Incorporate fermented foods such as kefir, yogurt, sauerkraut, and kimchi. Beneficial microorganisms found in these meals aid with digestion and intestinal health.

Seeds and Nuts:

Nutrient Snacking: Have a variety of nuts and seeds as a snack. They are a nutrient-dense snack choice since they are high in fiber, protein, healthy fats, vitamins, and minerals.

Include Seasonal Vegetables:

Seasonal Eating: To add diversity and freshness, embrace seasonal vegetables. Fruits and vegetables that are in season tend to have higher taste and nutritious content.

Techniques in Cooking:

Investigate Different Cooking Methods: Try out different cooking methods including grilling, roasting, steaming, and raw preparations. Foods may have their tastes and textures improved by a variety of techniques.

Exploration of World Cuisine:

Discover the flavors of the globe by tasting cuisines from various regions. Every country has distinctive ingredients and cooking customs that may enhance the variety of your meals.

Whole Food Munchies:

Snacking Wisely: Go for whole, high-nutrient snacks like a handful of almonds, fresh fruit, or veggies with hummus. These snacks don't depend on processed foods and instead improve overall nutrition.

Conscious Eating Techniques:

Make attentive Eating Choices: Be attentive of the foods you choose to consume. Making a conscious effort to vary the items you eat contributes to a varied and well-balanced diet.

Turn Over Meal Items:

Rotate the components of your meals by serving them in various ways. To provide diversity and avoid nutritional monotony, for instance, alternate your protein sources, grains, and veggies on a regular basis.

Personalized for Preferences:

Tailored Options: Adjust your meals according to nutritional requirements, cultural influences, or personal tastes. Maintaining a varied and pleasurable eating regimen is made simpler with this method.

By adopting these techniques, you may develop a diverse and well-rounded diet that increases taste sensations, encourages balanced nutrition, and supports general health and wellbeing.

CHAPTER SEVEN

Emotional Balance and Consumption

Emotional well-being and eating habits have a complicated and often linked connection. The capacity to recognize, control, and communicate emotions in a healthy manner is referred to as emotional wellbeing. The following are some ways that eating habits might affect emotional wellbeing and vice versa:

Emotional Consumption:

Coping Mechanism: When people turn to food as a way to manage stress, worry, depression, or other emotions, it's known as emotional eating. When faced with emotional anguish, people may resort to food for solace or as a diversion.

Consciously Consuming Food:

Conscious Food Choices: Mindful eating has a good effect on

eating habits when it comes to emotional wellbeing. Making deliberate eating decisions based on hunger and nutritional demands instead of emotional impulses is made possible by emotional awareness.

Eating under stress:

Impact on Food Choices: People who experience high levels of stress may turn to stress eating, which involves consuming comfort foods that are heavy in fat or sugar as a way to decompress. Emotional wellness techniques may assist manage stress and lessen the propensity to turn to bad eating habits.

Disorder of Binge Eating:

Emotional Component: Eating excessive amounts of food quickly is a symptom of binge eating disorder, which is often motivated by emotions. Counseling or therapy are examples of emotional health therapies that may help control and lessen binge eating episodes.

Using Your Innate Tastebuds

Understanding Your Body's Signals: Intuitive eating is supported by emotional wellbeing, which creates a link between feelings and bodily experiences. By paying attention to the body's signals of hunger and fullness, this method encourages a more harmonious relationship with food.

Self-Control:

Emotional Control: People who possess high emotional

health abilities are able to control their emotions more effectively and abstain from eating. Impulsive or emotional eating is less likely when emotional management is practiced.

Food as a Penalty or Reward:

Relationships with Emotions: People's perceptions of food are influenced by their emotional well-being, which determines whether they see it as a reward for good feelings or a punishment for bad ones. It's important to separate food from emotional rewards or penalties in order to have a positive connection with it.

Healthy Emotional Body Image:

Impact on Eating habits: Emotional well-being lowers the risk of restricted or unhealthy eating habits brought on by negative emotions or body dissatisfaction by promoting a positive body image.

Emotional and Social Link:

Social Eating: Social interactions, such as meals, and emotions are often entwined. People's strategies for navigating social eating are influenced by their emotional wellbeing, which helps to ensure that it stays a pleasurable and stress-free experience.

Cultural and affective factors:

Cultural Practices: Emotional well-being and eating habits may be influenced by cultural variables. Fostering a strong connection with one's background and traditional cuisine, as well as recognizing and enjoying the cultural characteristics of food, are all important components of being emotionally well-adjusted.

Therapeutic Strategies:

Counseling and Therapy: Emotional triggers linked to unhealthy eating patterns may be addressed by therapeutic treatments that improve emotional wellbeing, such as mindfulness-based therapies or cognitive-behavioral therapy (CBT).

Food's Emotional Satisfaction:

Emotionally well-being permits people to enjoy eating in moderation, but not to the exclusion of other sources of happiness and contentment. It encourages eating in moderation as a component of general wellbeing.

Emotional Hardiness:

Coping Mechanisms: A vital element of emotional wellbeing, emotional resilience provides people with useful coping mechanisms that don't only depend on food. This resilience enables one to deal with difficult emotions without turning to bad eating habits.

Effects of Dietary Decisions on Emotions:

Eating a Nutrient-Rich Diet: Eating a healthy diet may have a favorable effect on emotional wellbeing. Foods high in nutrients promote neurotransmitter function and brain health, which affect mood and emotional wellbeing.

Developing a positive connection with food requires an

understanding of and attention to the interaction between eating and emotional well-being. A more well-rounded and nutritious attitude to eating may be achieved via methods including practicing mindfulness, developing emotional regulation skills, and getting help from mental health specialists.

How to Identify Emotional Eating Triggers in a Practical Way

Identifying the things that set off emotional eating is a critical first step in creating a more positive relationship with food. The following are useful strategies for recognizing and resolving emotional eating triggers:

Maintain a Food Journal:

Keep Track of Emotional States: Keep a food journal in which you record your feelings both before and after meals. This may be used to find trends and linkages between certain emotions and eating habits.

Take a Moment to Think Before You Eat:

Check-in with Yourself: Give yourself a time to consider your emotional condition before reaching for food. Consider if you are indeed hungry or whether your need to eat may be the result of an emotional reaction.

Differentiate Between Emotional and Physical Hunger:

Body Language: Acquire the ability to discriminate between physiological and psychological hunger. Physical signs such as a rumbling stomach are often present when physical hunger develops gradually. Emotional hunger is often associated with certain emotions and may strike at any time.

Determine Particular Triggers:

Observe Patterns: Keep an eye out for circumstances, happenings, or feelings that often come before periods of emotional eating. You can deal with triggers more skillfully if you can identify their specifics.

Check-In on Emotions:

Frequent Self-Reflection: Plan frequent times throughout the day to check in emotionally. Evaluate your emotional condition and accept any tension, ennui, melancholy, or other feelings that could be there. Having this understanding may assist you in making thoughtful food decisions.

Conscious Eating Techniques:

Involve Your Senses: When eating, use your senses to cultivate mindful eating. Take note of your food's tastes, textures, and colors. You may avoid utilizing food as a means of emotional diversion and remain in the now by doing this.

Create Well-Being Coping Strategies:

Alternative Strategies: Create a toolkit of different ways to cope with emotions. This might include doing exercises like writing, deep breathing, conversing with friends, or pursuing a hobby.

Writing a Journal:

Expressive Writing: Using a journal to explore and express your feelings may be a very effective strategy. Write down your thoughts, worries, and experiences to have a better understanding of what could cause emotional eating.

Seek Expert Assistance:

Therapy or Counseling: You should think about getting help from a mental health expert if you find it difficult to control your emotional eating on your own. Tools and techniques for addressing underlying emotional problems may be obtained via therapy.

Create a Schedule:

Structured Eating Routine: Creating a consistent eating schedule helps reduce emotional-driven impulsive eating. Set aside time for meals and snacks at regular intervals to establish structure.

Relationship with Others:

Reach Out to Others: When you're feeling difficult emotions, get in touch with friends, relatives, or a support group. Speaking with others may help avoid resorting to food for consolation and provide emotional support.

Meditation with mindfulness:

Techniques for Mindfulness: To become more conscious of your thoughts and feelings without passing judgment, try mindfulness meditation. This may improve your capacity to react to emotions without becoming emotional.

Assess Outside Cues:

Determine Environmental Triggers: Examine your environment for any possible triggers, including locations, events, or even certain foods. Making deliberate decisions is made easier when you are aware of these outside stimuli.

Honor Non-Food Accomplishments:

Change the Focus: Honor non-food accomplishments or milestones rather than utilizing food as a consolation or reward. This facilitates the disassociation of food and emotions.

Have Reasonable Expectations:

Be Kind to Yourself: Recognize that everyone sometimes overeats due to emotions. Instead of concentrating on your perceived shortcomings, practice self-compassion and concentrate on creating more effective coping strategies.

Understanding oneself, practicing mindfulness, and being open to addressing underlying emotional problems are necessary to identify emotional eating triggers. You may improve the way you react to your emotions and increase your awareness of them by using these useful techniques.

Creating Effective Coping Mechanisms

Effective stress management and negotiating life's obstacles need the use of coping mechanisms. Creating adaptable reactions to different circumstances, building emotional resilience, and advancing general wellbeing are all components of developing effective coping methods. We'll go over essential ideas and doable actions for creating constructive coping mechanisms in this synopsis.

Comprehending Coping Mechanisms:

Different Coping Mechanism Types:

Problem-Focused: Techniques that deal with stress at its source.

Emotion-Focused: Stress management techniques for controlling emotional reactions.

Avoidance: Getting rid of stresses to temporarily relieve them.

Quick vs. Extended Coping:

Distinguish between tactics that promote long-term well-being and those that provide instant relief in order to achieve sustainable wellness.

Recognizing Your Own Stressors:

Introspection

Examining Personal Triggers: Determine certain pressures and triggers particular to your situation and way of life.

Awareness of Emotions:

Acknowledging Emotional Reactions: Recognize how stress affects emotions and how that affects wellbeing.

Positive Coping Principles:

Flexibility:

Flexibility in Responses: Practice flexibility in handling stresses, understanding that successful coping may call for modifying tactics.

A proactive mindset

Taking on Challenges Head-On: Adopt a proactive mentality to take on obstacles head-on and look for answers rather than wallowing in them.

Social Assistance:

Creating a Support System: To exchange experiences and get perspective, cultivate relationships with friends, family, or support groups.

Useful Techniques:

Techniques for Relaxation and Mindfulness:

Meditation & Mindful Breathing: Use mindfulness techniques to reduce stress and remain in the now.

Exercise:

Exercise as a Stress Reliever: Get regular exercise to boost endorphin production and lower stress levels.

Writing with Expression:

Journaling as a Way to Process Emotions and Get Clarity on Stressors: Write expressively in your journal to process your feelings.

Effective Time Management:

Setting Task Priorities: Learn efficient time management techniques to lessen overload and foster a sense of control.

Restructuring cognition:

Challenging Negative Thoughts: To promote a more optimistic outlook, reframe negative thinking patterns via cognitive restructuring.

Establishing Limits:

Setting Healthy limits: To safeguard your wellbeing and prevent needless stress, learn to create limits.

Interests and Creative Activities:

Fostering Passion Projects: Take up hobbies or artistic endeavors as a constructive way to decompress.

Getting Past Obstacles to Positive Coping:

Self-Empathy:

Cultivating Self-Love: Recognize that everyone has difficulties and use self-compassion to overcome obstacles.

Expert Assistance:

Therapeutic Interventions: To address the underlying causes of stress, seek professional assistance via counseling or therapy.

Tracking Development:

Contemplative Methodology:

Evaluate Coping Strategies: Consistently assess the efficacy of coping mechanisms and make necessary adjustments in response to feedback and experiences.

Getting Knowledge from Failures:

Resilience in the Face of Difficulties: See failures as chances for development, education, and the improvement of coping techniques.

In summary:

Creating healthy coping mechanisms is a continuous process that calls for self-awareness, dedication, and an openness to trying out different approaches. Through accepting flexibility, looking for social support, and using useful techniques, people may develop resilience and deal with life's challenges in a positive and capable way.

CHAPTER EIGHT

Exercise and Hunger

There are several variables that might affect the complex link between hunger and physical exercise. The following are important facets of the relationship between hunger and physical activity:

Short-Term Repression of Appetite:

Direct Effect: Physical exertion ranging from mild to vigorous might lower hunger temporarily. Hormonal changes, such as a rise in catecholamines and a fall in the hunger hormone ghrelin, are partially to blame for this transient drop in appetite.

Energy Outlay:

Caloric Balance: Physical exercise increases the body's total energy use. Exercise may provide a calorie deficit, which may result in weight reduction, depending on how intense and long it is. To reestablish energy balance, the body could react by boosting hunger, nonetheless.

Control of Hormones:

Leptin and Insulin: Exercise on a regular basis has been shown to have a good impact on the control of hormones, namely leptin and insulin sensitivity. The satiety hormone, leptin, assists the brain in detecting fullness. Better control over appetite may also be attributed to increased insulin sensitivity.

Personal Differences

Variations in Response: There may be differences in how an individual's hunger and physical activity are related. After exercising, some individuals could temporarily lose their appetite, while others might not notice any noticeable changes.

Timing of Exercise and Appetite:

Post-Exercise hunger: Different factors may affect hunger depending on when exercise occurs in relation to meals. Some people may feel more hungry after working out, particularly if they work out for a long time or really intensely.

Influence of Hydration:

Fluid Balance: Exercise may lead to increased perspiration and fluid loss, and the body may mistakenly perceive dehydration for hunger. It's critical to maintain hydration in order to recognize hunger cues and avoid overindulging.

Exercise Type and Intensity:

High-intensity vs low-intensity exercise: There are differences in the effects of exercise on hunger. While lower-intensity exercises may have a more subtle impact, high-intensity exercise may have a more potent short-term appetite suppressant.

Psychological Elements:

Mind-Body Connection: A major influence is exerted by psychological elements. Some people may get more hungry as a result of the psychological benefits of exercise, such as a feeling of achievement or actions motivated by incentives.

Frequent Activity and Controlling Appetite:

Long-Term Adaptations: Studies have shown a connection between consistent exercise and long-term enhancements in hunger control. Over time, regular exercise may help with improved weight control and more balanced appetite.

Reimbursement Dining:

Caloric Compensation: Eating extra food may be an instinctive way for some individuals to make up for the calories they burn off when exercising. The calorie loss brought on by physical exercise may be made up for by this compensation.

Personal Objectives and Type of Exercise:

Muscle Building vs. Weight Loss: The objectives of exercise, whether they be to gain muscle mass or lose weight, might affect how the hunger reacts. For instance, those who work out to gain muscle may find that their hunger increases in order to aid with muscle development and recuperation.

Timing of Nutrients After Exercise:

Effects of Nutrient Timing: Eating a well-balanced post-workout meal or snack that contains carbs and protein may have an impact on hunger. Timing of nutrients might influence recuperation and perhaps regulate hunger responses.

In order to control weight, enhance general health, or maximize athletic performance, people must comprehend how physical activity and hunger interact. It's important to acknowledge individual differences and take into account a comprehensive strategy that include mindful eating and exercise.

Exercise as a Healthy Living Catalyst

Because exercise improves one's physical, mental, and emotional health, it acts as a motivator for leading a healthy lifestyle. This is an investigation into the ways that physical activity promotes a healthy lifestyle:

Advantages for Physical Health:

Controlling Weight:

Caloric Expenditure: Exercise on a regular basis increases caloric expenditure, which helps control weight and lowers the risk of health problems associated with obesity.

Heart Health:

Heart Strength: By enhancing circulation, decreasing blood pressure, and reducing the risk of heart disease, cardiovascular workouts like cycling or jogging improve heart health.

Strength and Flexibility of Muscles:

Increased Mobility: Strength training activities lower the chance of injury and enhance everyday activities by promoting muscular development, flexibility, and support general mobility.

Bone Density:

Bone Health: Walking and resistance training are examples of weight-bearing workouts that increase bone density and lower the risk of osteoporosis and fractures.

Health of the Metabolic Process:

Blood Sugar Regulation: Exercise improves insulin sensitivity, which lowers the risk of type 2 diabetes and helps to better regulate blood sugar.

Enhanced Immune Response:

Support for the immunological System: Frequent moderate-intensity exercise has been associated with enhanced immunological function, which lowers the risk of illnesses.

Advantages for Mental Health

Reducing Stress:

Exercise reduces stress and fosters a feeling of relaxation and well-being by helping to control cortisol levels.

Mood Improvement

Endorphin produce: Exercise causes the body to produce endorphins, which are natural mood enhancers that help people feel better and fight symptoms of anxiety and sadness.

Mental Process:

Brain Health: Physical activity lowers the risk of age-related cognitive decline and supports cognitive function via neuroprotective effects.

Restful Sleep:

Sleep Patterns: Frequent exercise enhances the quality of sleep and helps reduce insomnia symptoms, both of which are beneficial to mental health in general.

Enhanced Vitality:

Enhanced Vitality: Physical exercise on a regular basis increases energy levels, preventing weariness and improving general vitality.

Emotional Health:

Self-Respect and Selfassurance:

Body Image Improvement: Reaching fitness objectives via exercise may improve one's sense of self-worth, appearance, and confidence in general.

Relationship with Others:

Community Engagement: Team sports and group workouts provide chances for social contact that build a feeling of belonging.

Emotional Hardiness:

Stress Coping Mechanism: Engaging in regular exercise promotes emotional resilience and offers a healthy way to deal with stress and hardship.

Prolonged Well-being and Illness Avoidance:

Prevention of Chronic Diseases:

Decreased chance: Engaging in regular physical exercise has been linked to a decreased chance of developing chronic illnesses including diabetes, cardiovascular disease, and certain types of cancer.

Proper Aging:

Sustaining Functionality: Physical activity promotes healthy aging by maintaining bone density, muscular mass, and cognitive abilities, all of which enhance general vitality as we age.

Integrating a Lifestyle:

Comprehensive Method:

Balanced Lifestyle: Exercise encourages people to embrace better habits including stress reduction, hydration, and a balanced diet by promoting a holistic approach to health.

Prolonged Devotion:

Exercise on a regular basis promotes the formation of sustainable lifestyle habits, which in turn creates a positive feedback loop that enhances one's health and overall well-being.

Exercise essentially influences several facets of mental, emotional, and physical wellness, acting as a catalyst. It creates the groundwork for a long and healthy life in addition to improving immediate well-being. Maintaining general health and vigor becomes largely dependent on incorporating regular physical exercise into everyday activities.

Exercise and Appetite Interaction

Exercise and hunger are intricately linked and include a number of physiological, psychological, and hormonal aspects. For those looking to control their weight, maintain their fitness objectives, or change to a healthier lifestyle, it might be important to understand how exercise affects hunger. Here are a few things to think about

Immediate Repercussions:

Suppression of Appetite:

Immediate Effect: Excessive or protracted exercise may cause a transient appetite suppression. Increased catecholamines (such adrenaline) and lowered ghrelin (the hunger hormone) during and just after exercise are often blamed for this effect.

Thirst and Hydration:

Fluid Balance: Sweating during exercise may cause an increase in fluid loss, and the body may mistake dehydration for hunger. Maintaining proper hydration is essential for correctly interpreting hunger cues.

Control of Hormones:

Sensitivity to Insulin and Leptin:

Exercise on a regular basis may have a good impact on the regulation of hormones, namely insulin sensitivity and leptin, the satiety hormone. Improved control over hunger is correlated with increased leptin sensitivity.

Ghrelin Concentrations:

activity and Ghrelin: Although ghrelin levels normally fall with activity, there may be variances depending on length, intensity, and personal reactions. Comprehending these subtleties helps in interpreting variations in hunger that occur after exercise.

Energy Billing and Reimbursement:

Calorie Consumption:

Energy Balance: Burning calories via exercise is essential for controlling weight. To restore energy balance, the body may, nevertheless, increase hunger in response to increased energy expenditure.

Consumption of Energy After Exercise:

Compensatory Eating: Some people may eat extra food inadvertently to make up for the calories they burn off while exercising. The calorie loss brought about by the activity may be offset by this compensation.

Exercise Type and Intensity:

Comparing High and Low Intensities:

Exercise Intensity and hunger: Exercises that are higher in intensity have the potential to suppress hunger more strongly in the near term than exercises that are lower in intensity. Individual reactions might differ, however.

Resistance vs. Aerobic Training:

Differential Effects: various forms of exercise, including strength training and aerobic exercises, might affect hunger in various ways. Compared to aerobic exercise, resistance training could be less likely to decrease hunger.

Psychological Elements:

Psychological Benefits:

Mood and Appetite: Exercise's positive psychological impacts, such a lifted mood and a feeling of achievement, might affect hunger. For some people, the psychological benefits of exercise may lead to an increase in hunger.

Conscious Eating Techniques:

Conscious Eating: Regardless of the effects of exercise, engaging in mindful eating, which is being present throughout meals, might assist people in better identifying signals of hunger and fullness.

When to Work Out and Eat:

Timing of Nutrients After Exercise:

Effects of Meal Timing: Eating a well-balanced meal or snack that includes carbs and protein after doing out may have an impact on your hunger thereafter. Timing of nutrients may affect appetite control and recuperation.

Before-Workout Diet:

Eating Before Exercise: Having an empty stomach while exercising might make you feel more hungry afterwards. Before working out, having a small meal or snack might help control your hunger afterward.

Personal Differences:

Personal and Genetic Factors:

Individual Reactions: Genetics, metabolic rate, body composition, and personal preferences may all have an impact on how each individual reacts to exercise and how it affects their hunger.

Evolution Through Time

Training Adaptations: Over time, individuals who exercise regularly may see changes in how their hunger is regulated. It is essential to comprehend these changes in order to keep intake and expenditure of energy in a healthy balance.

Effects Over Time:

Frequent Workout and Managing Your Weight:

Sustainable Habits: Including regular exercise in one's lifestyle encourages the formation of long-lasting habits that improve general health and long-term weight control.

Changes in Body Composition:

Impact of Muscle Mass: Long-term appetite management may be impacted by the metabolic effects of resistance exercise on an individual's growing muscle mass.

In conclusion, there are a variety of elements that impact the dynamic relationship between hunger and exercise. Exercise might help suppress hunger temporarily, but it's important to take into account individual reactions, different forms of exercise, and long-term adaptations. A conscious diet combined with physical exercise promotes general health and wellbeing.

CHAPTER NINE

Useful Advice for Daily Life

Many tactics that support general well-being, productivity, and a satisfying lifestyle are included in practical advice for daily living. Here are some useful advice for several facets of everyday life:

Well-being and Health:

Maintain Hydration:

Water Intake: To keep hydrated, support numerous body processes, and promote general health, drink enough water throughout the day.

Healthy Eating:

Diverse Diet: Eat a diet rich in whole grains, fruits, vegetables, lean meats, and healthy fats. Make sure your diet is balanced and diverse. Strive for portion management and moderation.

Frequent Exercise:

Include Movement: Look for chances to move throughout the day, such as walks on a regular basis, workout regimens, or physically demanding hobbies. Regular exercise promotes both mental and physical health.

Sufficient Sleep:

Quality Rest: Make sleep a priority by setting up a regular sleep schedule and a calming nighttime ritual. Good sleep is essential for mental clarity and general wellbeing.

Efficiency and Structure:

Set Task Priorities:

Task management: Set priorities for your tasks by using to-do lists or task management software. Prioritize your tasks in order to increase output.

Blocking out time:

A structured schedule should use time blocking to set out certain time slots for various tasks. This supports sustained attention and efficient time management.

Clear Out Areas:

Organized Environments: To establish a space that is both orderly and productive, frequently declutter your home and place of employment.

Establish sensible objectives:

Realistic and Achievable Goals: Define your objectives and divide them up into smaller, more manageable activities. Honor accomplishments, no matter how little.

Emotional and Mental Health:

Put mindfulness into practice:

Present Moment Awareness: To relieve stress and improve mental clarity, include mindfulness exercises into your everyday routine, such as mindful walking, meditation, or deep breathing.

Establish Social Connections:

Sustain Relationships: Encourage social interactions by staying in touch with friends and family on a regular basis. Emotional health is influenced by social relationships.

Show Your Appreciation:

Gratitude diary: Review the good things in your life in your gratitude diary. Developing thankfulness may improve pleasure in general.

Limit the amount of time spent on screens:

Establish screen time limits as part of your digital detox, particularly before bed. Electronic gadget breaks are beneficial to mental health.

Accounting for Finances:

Setting a budget:

Financial Planning: To efficiently manage spending, create

and adhere to a budget. Keep tabs on your spending patterns to find possible places to save money.

Emergency Reserve:

Financial Security: Set aside money for unforeseen costs by creating an emergency fund. Peace of mind is derived from having a safety net for finances.

Invest Sensibly:

Long-Term Planning: Think about long-term financial objectives and investigate investment choices. If necessary, seek expert guidance to make well-informed judgments.

Self-Helding:

Personal Time:

Personal Breaks: Set aside time for enjoyable and calming self-care activities. This may include taking a leisurely bath, reading, or engaging in hobbies.

Acquire the Ability to Say No:

Establishing healthy boundaries and learning when to say no are important. Self-care should be prioritized; do not overcommit.

Frequent Medical Examinations:

Preventive Care: Make time for regular exams to keep an eye on your health and take care of any possible issues before they become serious.

Ongoing Education:

Read Often:

Lifelong Learning: Make reading a regular habit. Books, articles, or instructional materials that promote lifelong learning might be used.

Enhancement of Skills:

Online Courses: Take advantage of online seminars or courses to expand your skill set and keep current in your career or personal endeavors.

Request Input:

Be Receptive to Input: Keep an open mind and actively look for methods to do better. Personal development is facilitated by ongoing learning and development.

Accountability for the Environment:

Trim, Reuse, and Recycle

Sustainable Practices: To support environmental sustainability, develop eco-friendly behaviors including cutting down on single-use plastics, recycling, and trash reduction.

Save Energy:

Energy Efficiency: When not in use, switch off lights and appliances to save energy. When combined, little actions have a big effect.

Keep in mind that you may modify these suggestions to fit your own needs and tastes. The possibility of long-lasting good changes in your daily life is increased when you form habits that are consistent with your beliefs and objectives.

Portion management and thoughtful serving

The concepts of portion management and mindful serving center on controlling the amount of food you consume and paying attention to your dining experience. These routines may help with weight control, improved health, and cultivating a more thoughtful relationship with food.

Control of Portion:

Comprehending Portion Sizes

Serving Sizes: Acquire knowledge of the typical serving sizes for various food categories. This keeps you from overindulging and lets you enjoy a range of meals in moderation

Employ Measuring Equipment:

Kitchen Utensils: When cooking at home, measure servings with measuring cups, spoons, or a food scale. This guarantees that serving sizes and calorie consumption are accurate.

Visual Indications:

Portion Size Estimation: Gain proficiency in visually estimating portion sizes over time. A serving of protein, for instance, is about the size of a deck of cards.

Steer clear of super-sizing:

Avoid Upsizing: When eating out, avoid the urge to get bigger amounts. Choose regular or reduced portions to control your caloric intake.

Distribute Greater Portions:

Dining Out Strategy: To manage portion sizes and lower calorie intake, think about splitting dishes with friends or family if restaurant portions are substantial.

Cautious Serving:

Be Aware of Hunger Cues:

Pay Attention to Your Body: Adjust serving sizes to suit your level of hunger. Be mindful of your body's fullness cues and refrain from overindulging.

Make Use of Smaller Plates:

Optical illusion: To give the impression of larger portions, use smaller bowls and plates. You may feel more content with smaller portions as a result of this.

Serve Cautiously:

Conscious Decisions: Take care while preparing meals. Make sure your plate is well-balanced, with a range of colors and food categories, and take into account the nutritional value of each component.

Pre-portioning meals:

Plan Ahead: Whenever feasible, portion meals and snacks ahead of time. By doing this, you may manage portion sizes before sitting down to eat and avoid mindless munching.

Keep Your Meals Out of Packages:

Avoid mindless snacking by not eating straight out of big bags or containers. To avoid overindulging, divide food into smaller portions instead.

Enjoy Every Bite:

Eat Slowly: Savor each meal by taking your time. Eating slowly lessens the chance of overeating since it enables your body to detect fullness signals.

Involve Your Senses:

Savor Textures and Flavors: Use all of your senses while you eat. Pay attention to the tastes, textures, and scents of your food, fostering a more joyful and complete dining experience.

Conscientious Eating Setting:

Distraction-Free Zone: Keep distractions like TV and electronics out of the dining room to foster mindfulness. Pay attention to the food and the eating process.

The Mixture of Both:

Harmony and Pleasure:

Moderation: A balanced approach to eating is encouraged when portion management and mindful serving are combined. You don't have to feel deprived to enjoy a wide range of meals.

Develop Sensitivity:

Conscious Choices: Mindful serving and portion management work together to create knowledge about food choices, which promotes a positive connection with eating.

Stop Overindulging:

Avoiding Excess: You may avoid overindulging and encourage a feeling of contentment with sensible serving sizes by paying attention to portion sizes and the process of serving.

A deliberate and thoughtful approach to eating is encouraged by both mindful serving and quantity management. They enable people to make knowledgeable decisions about what and how much they eat, promoting a more thoughtful and health-conscious way of living.

Appropriate Snacking to Maintain Energy

A useful and practical suggestion for daily life is to snack wisely for prolonged energy. This may assist to maintain energy levels, balance blood sugar, and promote general well-being. Here's an explanation of what constitutes smart eating and how to include it into your daily schedule:

Comprehending Intelligent Snacking

Rich in Nutrients Options:

Balanced Nutrition: Select snacks that include a range of macronutrients, including healthy fats, carbs, and protein. Over time, energy levels are sustained by this balanced strategy.

Considerate Portions:

Controlled Servings: Take care while estimating portion

sizes to prevent consuming too many calories. Use little containers or portion foods ahead of time to avoid thoughtless overindulgence.

Foods High in Fiber:

Incorporate high-fiber snacks, such as fruits, vegetables, or whole grains, to promote satiety and digestive health. Fiber helps the digestive system and encourages fullness.

Options Packed with Protein:

Muscle Support: Include high-protein snacks such as almonds, Greek yogurt, and lean meats. Protein contributes to the maintenance of muscular mass and a long-lasting sensation of fullness.

Good Fats:

Incorporate foods high in healthy fats, including avocados, almonds, and seeds, for your brain and energy support. These lipids provide a slow-releasing energy source and promote brain function.

Minimal Added Sugars:

Stable Blood Sugar: To avoid sharp rises and falls in blood sugar, choose foods with less added sugar. When possible, use genuine fruit sweetness.

Useful Advice for Daily Life:

Organizing Snacks Ahead:

The secret is to prepare: make a plan for your snacks in advance, particularly on hectic days. This stops people from seeking for convenient but harmful choices.

Carrying Snacks:

Options for On-the-Go: Always have portable, non-perishable snacks on hand, including whole fruit, nuts, and seeds, or trail mix. This guarantees that you always have wise choices.

Drinking plenty of water

Water Intake: Drink plenty of water since sometimes people confuse dehydration for appetite. Snack on hydrating foods like fruits that are high in water content and sip water throughout the day.

When to Snack:

Regular Intervals: To ensure a consistent flow of energy, try to have snacks in between meals. An excessive amount of time between meals might cause energy dips and subsequent overeating.

Combining Different Food Groups:

The ideal snack mix is to blend many food categories together. For a well-rounded choice, try serving Greek yogurt with berries or apple slices with almond butter.

Steer clear of highly processed snacks:

Whole Foods Preferred: Reduce the amount of highly processed snacks, which are often devoid of nourishment and heavy in harmful fats and added sugars.

Pay Attention to Your Body:

Hunger Signals: Be aware of your body's signals of hunger and fullness. When you're really hungry, have a snack; when you're full, quit.

Variety Is Essential:

Diverse Options: To avoid boredom and guarantee a wide range of nutrients, have a variety of snacks on hand. Over time, this aids in meeting your nutritional demands as well.

Consciously Consuming Food:

Conscious Consumption: Take a thoughtful approach to eating by appreciating every taste. This makes snacking more enjoyable and promotes eating with greater awareness.

Personalized Snacks:

Controlled Ingredients: To have more control over ingredients, think about making your own snacks. This lets you customize your snacks to fit your dietary requirements.

Examples of Wise Snacks

Berries with Greek Yogurt with a Honey Drizzle:

Fiber, protein, and antioxidants.

Almond butter on sliced apples:

Fiber, protein, and healthy fats.

Sticks of vegetables with hummus:

Sturdy, Full of Protein and Nutrients.

Cheese with Whole Grain Cracker:

Whole grains, protein, and healthy fats.

Nuts and dried fruits in a trail mix:

Natural sugars, protein, and healthy fats.

Making deliberate food choices that fuel your body and maintain your energy levels throughout the day is the key to smart snacking for prolonged energy. These suggestions may help you maintain your general health and wellbeing by implementing them into your everyday routine.

CHAPTER TEN

Circadian Rhythms and Sleep

Circadian rhythms and sleep are related processes that are essential for controlling the body's many physiological and behavioral activities. It is essential to comprehend these ideas in order to support sound sleep habits and general wellbeing.

Rest:

Sleep is a restorative state that occurs naturally in cycles. It is during this time that the body goes through many physiological processes that are critical to both physical and mental health.

Sleep Stages:

NREM and REM: Non-Rapid Eye Movement (NREM) and Rapid Eye Movement (REM) are the two primary phases of sleep. Throughout the sleep cycle, each stage has unique traits and purposes.

Cycles of Sleep:

Repetitive Phases: A whole sleep cycle, which lasts between 90 and 110 minutes, is made up of many cycles of REM and NREM sleep. Throughout a normal sleep cycle, the body passes through these stages several times.

Sleep's purposes include:

Restoration and Maintenance: Sleep plays a critical role in immune system function, memory consolidation, emotional stability, and physical recovery. It promotes general well-being and helps maintain peak cognitive function.

Suitable Sleep Position:

Healthy Sleep Practices: Establishing a setting and forming routines that encourage restful sleep are important components of good sleep hygiene. This entails sticking to a regular sleep schedule, setting up a relaxing sleeping space, and abstaining from stimulants just before bed.

The circadian rhythms

Definition:

Biological Clock: Roughly every 24 hours, internal, natural processes known as circadian rhythms occur. They control body temperature, hormone production, sleep-wake cycles, and other physiological processes.

SCN, or suprachiasmatic nucleus:

Master Clock: The brain's hypothalamic suprachiasmatic

nucleus acts as the body's master clock, regulating circadian rhythms in response to external stimuli, mostly light.

Outside Factors:

Light and Darkness: Exposure to light affects circadian rhythms primarily. The body's internal clock is synchronized when it is exposed to natural light during the day and restricted artificial light at night.

Cycle of Sleep and Wakefulness:

Day and Night Synchronization: Circadian rhythms affect how long people sleep and wake up, naturally increasing alertness throughout the day and decreasing drowsiness at night.

Control of Temperature:

Fluctuations During the Day: The 24-hour cycle naturally causes a rise and fall in body temperature, which is also influenced by circadian rhythms. Changes in temperature affect both alertness and sleepiness.

Control of Hormones

Melatonin and Cortisol: The release of these two hormones is influenced by circadian cycles. Cortisol levels rise in the morning, encouraging alertness, while melatonin, which promotes sleep, is normally secreted more in the evening.

Circadian Rhythms and Sleep Interaction:

Harmonization:

Alignment for Optimal Function: Circadian rhythms and the

sleep-wake cycle must be in sync for healthy sleep. Overall wellbeing and the quality of sleep are enhanced when these systems are in harmony.

Shift Work with Jet Lag:

Disruptions and Adjustments: Temporary sleep disruptions may result from jet lag, which is the crossing of time zones, or shift work, which is the working at irregular hours.

Biological Clock Difference

Individual Variations: Different individuals have different circadian rhythms; some are "morning people" (morning chronotypes) by nature, while others are "night owls" (evening chronotypes).

Effect on Well-Being:

disturbances and Health Risks: People who work shifts or have irregular sleep cycles may be at a higher risk of developing chronic circadian rhythm disturbances, which may lead to metabolic diseases, cardiovascular problems, and cognitive decline.

Light Exposition and Sleep Departure:

Melatonin Release: Keeping circadian rhythms and sleep-wake cycles in sync is facilitated by exposing oneself to natural light during the day and limiting artificial light at night. Evening light exposure may inhibit the production of melatonin, which delays the start of sleep.

Promoting a healthy and regular sleep pattern requires an understanding of and respect for the interaction between circadian rhythms and sleep. The alignment of these essential processes for general well-being is facilitated by consistent sleep patterns, exposure to natural light throughout the day, and the creation of a sleep-friendly atmosphere.

Effects of Sleep on Regulating Appetite

Sleep is important for controlling appetite because it affects signals of hunger and fullness. Sleep disturbances or insufficient sleep length may affect the hormones and neurotransmitters that regulate hunger, which may result in changes in eating habits. The following are some major effects of sleep on controlling appetite:

Levels of Ghrelin and Leptin:

Hormone of Hunger (Ghrelin): Lack of sleep has been linked to a rise in ghrelin, the hormone that triggers hunger. Ghrelin levels that are elevated might increase appetite and lead to overindulgence in food.

The hormone known as leptin, which indicates satiety and fullness, may, on the other hand, be less present in the body as a result of insufficient sleep. Weaker appetite suppression may be the outcome of decreased leptin levels.

A rise in the desire for foods high in calories:

Preference for High-Calorie, High-Carbohydrate meals: Lack of sleep has been associated with a greater appetite for high-calorie, high-carbohydrate meals. This inclination for meals high in energy might be a factor in overindulging in calories.

Modifications to Insulin Sensitivity:

Insulin Resistance: Sleep deprivation may have an impact on insulin sensitivity in a manner similar to that of insulin-resistant people. This insulin-related dysfunction may be a factor in increased appetite and problems with glucose metabolism.

Stress Reaction and Emotional Eating:

Effect on Emotional Well-Being: Lack of sleep may lead to higher stress levels and problems regulating emotions. People may turn to food as a consolation while under stress, leading to emotional eating.

Circadian rhythm disruption:

Circadian Misalignment: Disturbances in sleep patterns or circadian rhythms, such working shifts or experiencing jet lag, may cause a disruption in the usual timing of hormone release, which can have an impact on metabolic processes and hunger control.

Increasing Energy Consumption:

Total Calorie Consumption: Research indicates that those who don't get enough sleep could eat more calories overall, especially from snacks. Over time, this increased calorie consumption may lead to weight gain.

Effect on Controlling Weight:

Risk of Obesity: Long-term sleep deprivation has been linked to a higher chance of obesity. Difficulties in maintaining a healthy weight may be attributed to both inadequate sleep length and poor sleep quality.

Impact on Nutritional Decisions:

Change in Food Preferences: People who don't get enough sleep may have a predilection for foods with greater energy content and bigger servings. An imbalance in the amount of calories consumed may result from this change in eating preferences.

Decision-Making Impairment:

Effects on cognition: Not getting enough sleep might affect how well one thinks, which includes making decisions about what to eat. People who don't get enough sleep may be more impulsive and less inclined to choose healthful foods.

Connectivity to Metabolic Disorders:

Type 2 Diabetes and Cardiovascular Risk: Sleep disruptions have been associated, in part because of their impact on appetite management and metabolic health, with a higher risk of developing type 2 diabetes and cardiovascular disorders.

Understanding how sleep affects hunger management emphasizes how crucial it is to prioritize maintaining regular sleep patterns and practicing excellent sleep hygiene for general health and wellbeing. A suitable sleep environment, regular bedtimes, and getting enough sleep are just a few of the healthy sleep practices that may help you achieve your weight management objectives and improve hunger control.

How to Create Healthy Sleep Patterns in a Practical Way

Creating an atmosphere that supports restful sleep and establishing regular behaviors are essential to establishing good sleep patterns. The following are doable strategies to encourage and sustain sound sleep:

Regular Sleep Schedule:

Establish Regular Bedtimes and Wake Times: Even on the weekends, maintain a regular sleep routine by going to bed and getting up at the same times each day. This aids in the internal clock regulation of your body.

Establish a Calm Bedtime Schedule:

Wind Down Routines: Establish peaceful bedtime routines, such as reading a book, having a warm bath, or using relaxation methods. Your body receives this signal from these actions to wind down.

Enhance Your Sleep Environment

Comfy Bed and Bedding: Make a purchase of pillows and a comfy mattress. Make sure your bedroom is quiet, dark, and maintained at a nice, cozy temperature. If necessary, think about earplugs and blackout curtains.

Minimize Your Screen Time:

Reduce Blue Light: Give yourself at least an hour before bed to avoid using displays on computers, phones, or tablets. The hormone that promotes sleep, melatonin, may be inhibited by the blue light that electronic gadgets generate.

Be Aware of What You Eat and Drink:

Avoid Large Meals Right Before Bed: Try to finish your last meal two to three hours before going to bed. Caffeine and nicotine should be avoided in the hours before bed since they may interfere with sleep cycles.

Frequent Workout:

Include Physical Activity: Move around often, but steer clear of strenuous exercise just before bed. While vigorous activity in the late afternoon may have the opposite impact, moderate exercise may help improve sleep.

Control Your Anxiety and Stress:

Relaxation Techniques: Engage in stress-relieving exercises including gradual muscle relaxation, deep breathing, and meditation. Before going to bed, make a note of any worries so you can deal with them the following day.

Limit naps

Short and Early Naps: If you must take a sleep, plan it for early in the day and limit it to no more than twenty to thirty minutes. Avoid taking naps in the late afternoon since they might disrupt your sleep at night.

Make Use of the Bed for Sleeping:

Link Bed with Sleep: Only use your bed for sleeping and private moments. Do not use electronics in bed for business, watching TV, or utilizing other purposes. This facilitates the brain's association between sleep with the bed.

Allow Natural Light to Enter Your Body:

Day Exposure: Go outside throughout the course of the day. Being exposed to natural light throughout the day helps your body's internal clock to be more balanced.

Create a Calm Sleep Environment:

Investing in soft bedding can help you establish a pleasant sleeping environment. To lessen noise and block out outside light, think about using blackout curtains.

If Needed, Seek Professional Assistance:

Persistent Sleep Problems: If you follow these tactics but still have trouble falling asleep, you should see a doctor or a sleep expert for advice and assessment.

Lower Fluid Consumption Before Sleep:

Hydrate Earlier in the Day: By consuming less fluids in the evening, you may lower your chance of having to get up throughout the night to use the restroom. Instead, drink plenty of water throughout the day.

Create a Winding Down Schedule:

Calm and Mindful Activities: Spend the hour before sleep doing peaceful and thoughtful activities. This might be journaling, light stretching, or relaxing music listening.

Steer clear of stimulant substances:

Limit your consumption of nicotine and caffeinated drinks, particularly in the hours leading up to sleep. These drugs may make it difficult for you to fall asleep.

These useful suggestions will help you create and maintain appropriate sleep habits, which will enhance your general wellbeing and cognitive abilities. As consistency is essential, try incorporating these routines into your sleep schedule on a regular basis.

Section Eleven

Changes in a Sustainable Lifestyle

Sustainable lifestyle adjustments are adjustments to one's regular routines and behaviors that are socially and ecologically responsible in addition to being health-conscious. These adjustments are meant to lessen their negative effects on the environment, increase long-term well-being, and encourage a more sustainable and conscientious way of life. Changes to a sustainable lifestyle may be made in the following areas:

1. Nutrition and Diet:

Plant-Based Eating: Increase the amount of plant-based foods in your diet, with a focus on whole grains, fruits, vegetables, and legumes. Lowering meat intake may benefit the environment and human health, particularly if the meat comes from non-sustainable sources.

Local & Seasonal Foods: To lessen the carbon footprint involved in long-distance food transportation, buy seasonal vegetables and support your local farmers.

Minimize Food Waste: To reduce food waste, carefully plan your meals, store them, and repurpose them.

2. Eco-Friendly Style:

Sustainable and Ethical Clothes: Go for clothes made of eco-friendly materials, back companies that have ethical and transparent supply chains, and choose classic styles over fads.

Second-Hand Shopping: To lessen the need for new production, look through thrift stores, vintage shops, or internet marketplaces for used apparel and accessories.

Clothes Care: Preserve your clothes for a longer time by giving them the right attention, including air drying, mild cleaning, and patching rather than throwing away.

3. Cutting Down on Single-Use Items

Reusable Products: Water bottles, shopping bags, coffee cups, and cutlery are a few examples of reusable things that may take the place of single-use ones.

minimum Packaging: To cut down on waste, choose items with minimum or environmentally friendly packaging.

4. Energy Effectiveness:

Energy-saving tips include shutting off lights and appliances when not in use. Think about using lightbulbs and gadgets that use less energy.

Renewable Energy Sources: Look into ways to power your house with renewable energy sources like solar or wind.

5. Transport:

Sustainable Commuting: To lessen your carbon impact,

choose to walk, bike, carpool, or use public transit.

Fuel-Efficient automobiles: To reduce pollution, opt for electric or fuel-efficient automobiles wherever feasible.

6. Reducing Waste:

Composting: To cut down on the quantity of garbage dumped in landfills, begin composting organic waste.

Recycling: Learn the recycling regulations in your area and try to recycle correctly.

7. Consciously Use Water:

Water conservation may be achieved by utilizing water-saving equipment, sealing leaks, and paying attention to how much water is used at home.

Reducing Plastic Waste: Select goods that come in as little plastic packaging as possible and think about switching to reusable plastic products.

8. Utilizing Technology Mindfully:

Digital Minimalism: Choose sustainable tech items, minimize technological waste, and be careful of screen time while practicing digital minimalism.

Eco-Friendly Electronics: Look for electronics that have received eco-friendly certifications, and if possible, repair or rehabilitate existing equipment rather than buying new ones.

9. Participation in the Community:

Encourage Local activities: Participate in neighborhood campaigns to advance sustainability, lend your support to companies that practice eco-friendliness, and become active in local sustainability activities.

Educate and Act: Inform friends and family about sustainable behaviors and push for laws that support social responsibility and environmental preservation.

10. Happiness and Mindfulness:

Living Mindfully: Develop an awareness of your behaviors and how they affect the environment and your well-being by engaging in mindfulness practices.

Holistic Health: Make mental and emotional health a priority by engaging in practices like stress reduction, meditation, and building healthy relationships.

Making decisions that are in line with one's own well-being as well as the wellbeing of the environment is necessary for sustainable lifestyle adjustments. People may contribute to a more sustainable, responsible, and health-conscious style of living by implementing these changes into their everyday lives.

Creating Durable Routines for a Healthier Life

Developing tactics that encourage consistency and making small, sustainable improvements are key to creating enduring habits for a better lifestyle. The following useful advice may assist you in creating and sustaining healthy habits:

1. Begin Little:

Start with modest, doable adjustments. It might be daunting to attempt a complete lifestyle makeover all at once. Select one or two behaviors in particular to work on first.

2. Establish Specific, Achievable Goals:

Establish quantifiable, attainable, and unambiguous objectives. Make sure your goals are clear and that you divide more ambitious objectives into more manageable benchmarks.

3. Establish a Routine:

Introduce new routines into your everyday life. Establishing a schedule aids in ingraining these behaviors into your everyday life, which is crucial.

4. One habit at a time, pay attention:

To prevent wearing yourself out too much, focus on developing one habit at a time. You may progressively make more adjustments as a habit solidifies.

5. Link Routines to Current Cues:

Connect new behaviors to ingrained signals or patterns. For instance, just after brushing your teeth in the morning, stretch if you want to make it a regular habit.

6. Employ Triggers

Determine the cues that cause the intended action. This might be a particular moment of the day, an occasion, or an image that acts as a prompt to carry out the habit.

7. Monitor Your Development:

Document your progress and efforts. This might be a simple checklist, an app for recording habits, or a diary. Maintaining a record helps you feel accomplished and validates your dedication.

8. Honor minor victories:

Celebrate each little accomplishment you make along the road. Acknowledging your successes, no matter how little, increases drive and supports constructive behavior.

9. Expand on Achievement:

Use your first accomplishment in integrating a habit as a starting point for future endeavors. Create a good behavior chain by introducing new habits gradually.

10. Include Social Support:

Tell your loved ones, friends, or a support group about your objectives. Having a solid support system may help with motivation, accountability, and encouragement.

11. Imagine Your Success:

Imagine yourself carrying out the desired habit effectively. Visualization may help you stay motivated by helping you see the benefits of your work in your mind.

12. Adjust to Difficulties:

Anticipate difficulties and failures. Consider them as chances to grow and modify your strategy rather than as setbacks. Adaptability is essential to success in the long run.

13. Create a Healthful Environment:

Adjust your surroundings to assist your objectives. For instance, decrease the amount of bad snacks in your kitchen and fill it with wholesome items if you wish to follow a better diet.

14. Give Consistency More Weight Than Intensity:

Intensity is not as crucial as consistency. In the long run, consistent, moderate efforts outperform intermittent, strong spurts of exercise in terms of sustainability and effectiveness.

15. Exercise Forbearance:

It takes time to form habits. It takes time for change to occur, so be kind to yourself. Keep your attention on the adventure and resist the need for quick fixes.

16. Think and Modify:

Evaluate your progress on a regular basis and be prepared to modify your strategy if needed. Your objectives and circumstances could shift, necessitating a modification in your routine.

17. Consult a Professional:

For individualized direction and assistance, think about speaking with a coach or a health professional. They may provide you specialized guidance and support as you overcome obstacles.

You may create enduring habits that lead to a happier, healthier life by using these techniques and keeping an optimistic outlook. Keep in mind that adopting a healthy lifestyle is a continuous process, and every decision you make will get you one step closer to your long-term health objectives.

Overcoming Obstacles and Maintaining Motivation

Developing and sustaining good habits requires overcoming obstacles and being driven. The following techniques can assist you in overcoming challenges and maintaining motivation as you move toward a healthy lifestyle:

1. Determine Possible Difficulties:

Be prepared for obstacles that could arise. Being aware of possible roadblocks enables you to prepare ahead of time for solutions and avoid disappointments.

2. Create a Mindset for Solving Problems:

Take on obstacles by adopting a problem-solving perspective. Consider them as chances to come up with innovative solutions and get new insights about yourself rather than obstacles.

3. Set Smaller Steps Toward Your Objectives:

Divide highly ambitious objectives into smaller, more doable tasks. Reaching these little goals gives you a feeling of achievement and keeps you motivated.

4. Adjust Objectives as Needed:

Be adaptable in achieving your objectives. If you face unforeseen difficulties or circumstances change, think about modifying your objectives to be doable and realistic.

5. Establish a Support Network:

Be in the company of encouraging friends, relatives, or neighbors. By letting others know about your struggles and successes, you build a network of support and responsibility.

6. Consult a Professional:

Seek advice from coaches, therapists, or health experts if you are facing difficult issues. Their knowledge may provide customized plans for conquering certain challenges.

7. Acquire Knowledge from Failures:

See failures as stepping stones to success. Examine what went wrong, draw lessons from the event, and use the newfound understanding to modify your strategy going ahead.

8. Honor Advancement:

Honor all of your accomplishments, no matter how little. Acknowledging your success gives you more self-assurance and strengthens the excellent habits you've worked so hard to develop.

9. See the Long-Term Gains:

Remember the long-term advantages. Imagine how your efforts will improve your general quality of life, health, and wellbeing. This may be a very effective source of inspiration when things are tough.

10. Develop Your Own Motivation:

Make a connection with your inner motives and ideals. To create long-lasting motivation, realize why your objectives are important to you on a deeper level than just the outside world.

11. Use encouraging statements:

Affirmations and constructive self-talk are recommended. To increase confidence and have a positive outlook, remind yourself of your talents, strengths, and previous accomplishments.

12. Put in Place Rewards

Create a system of rewards for reaching certain objectives. Reward yourself with non-food items that support your objectives, like a rejuvenating spa day or a stylish exercise equipment.

13. Change Up Your Daily Schedule:

In order to avoid being bored, add variation to your routine. Trying different things keeps things fresh and might help you become excited about your healthy routines again.

14. Monitor Development:

Keep a regular record of your progress using notebooks, applications, or graphic charts. Seeing your accomplishments on paper may serve as a concrete record of your journey and serve as motivation.

15. Create Reliable Habits:

Give consistency priority above perfection. Long-term success is facilitated by the establishment of persistent habits, no matter how little.

16. Consider Your Why:

Regularly consider the motivations underlying your objectives. Making a connection with your "why" gives you a stronger feeling of purpose and deepens your dedication.

17. Put mindfulness into practice:

Include mindfulness exercises in your daily routine. You may make deliberate decisions that are in line with your objectives, manage stress, and remain present by practicing mindfulness.

18. Put Self-Care First:

Make sure you take care of yourself enough to keep your general health. Resilience and an optimistic outlook are enhanced by taking good care of your bodily and emotional well-being.

19. Adorn Yourself with Positive Encounters:

Embrace the wonderful forces that surround you. Restrict your exposure to unfavorable circumstances or influences that might sap your drive.

20. Review and Modify Objectives:

Review your objectives on a regular basis and adapt as necessary. Your objectives may need to alter as circumstances do in order to be relevant and reachable.

Recall that motivation is an ephemeral force that changes with time. You may overcome obstacles and keep up the drive required to create and maintain a healthy life by putting these techniques into practice and cultivating a resilient attitude.

CONCLUSION

A. Crucial Learning Points:

Several important lessons may be learned from controlling appetite for a healthy way of living. Recognizing appetite's intricate interactions with environmental, psychological, and physiological components is essential to understanding it. It's important to promote a thoughtful and balanced eating style in addition to just reducing hunger. This process includes learning to discern between feeding the body and sating appetites, as well as adopting mindful eating habits and identifying hunger and satisfaction indicators.

Crucial components include building a base of nutrient-dense meals, staying hydrated for health, and designing regular meal schedules. Adding diversity for balanced nutrition, realizing the influence of emotional wellbeing on eating, and comprehending the connection between exercise, physical activity, and hunger are all part of building on this foundation.

The investigation includes adjustments to sustainable lifestyles, stressing decisions that enhance individual welfare while taking society and environmental effects into account. In addition to personal behaviors, the pursuit of a healthy lifestyle also calls for support networks, community involvement, and mindfulness.

B. Motivating Readers to Master Their Appetite and Adopt a Healthier Lifestyle:

Making the decision to control your hunger and start living a healthy life is powerful. It's a call to change the way you feel about eating, take care of your body, and improve your general wellbeing. Gaining knowledge about the complexities of hunger gives you the power to make wise decisions, pay attention to your body's cues, and adopt a more mindful eating style.

This journey is about making a permanent lifestyle transformation, not about fast cures or restricted diets. It's a chance to enjoy the bounty of nutrient-dense foods, recognize the advantages of staying hydrated, and discover happiness in thoughtful, balanced eating. It's about forming enduring habits and laying the groundwork for health that sustains your physical, mental, and emotional well-being.

Remind yourself that every step you take ahead, no matter

how little, is a victory as you overcome obstacles and disappointments. Celebrate your accomplishments, draw lessons from your past, and develop a resilient attitude. Your journey to a healthy way of living is distinct, and the decisions you make have an impact on those around you as well as a healthier, more peaceful world.

So enjoy the process of becoming an appetite master. Accept the ability to fuel your mind, body, and spirit. As you do, you're embracing a life full of energy, well-being, and the satisfaction that comes with reaching your greatest potential — rather than merely changing your behaviors

ABOUT THE AUTHOR

About The Author BLESSED CHARLES Blessed Charles is a young and an enthusiastic person that is passionate about the wellbeing of individual around him and so endeavors to by all means possible drive home insights to achieve this.

He is a well-rounded and an informed educator, an environmentalist, a speaker as well as a lover of God. He is happily married.